"So real, so raw and so personal, an absolute joy ___ ___ ____ ead at the same time. You are so incredibly resilient and I'm so proud of you for taking this leap and sharing your story, it's so special and so important. You are one of a kind."

"Did NOT want to put it down! One of those books where I wanted to read it non-stop..."

"All I can say is so far, I completely understand every word you are saying. I feel your compassion for your mom and look forward to continuing this heartfelt read. Thank you for being so honest."

"To have someone who understands you. That you're not crazy and you're not alone. I can't explain. Every child of addiction should read this and realize they're not alone."

"And here's a family I always wished my family was – who had it all, out and open saying hey man we're not perfect, it's hard, and if you don't like it, fuck off – Empowering. Thank you."

"Through the author's masterful storytelling, readers are taken on an emotional roller-coaster, witnessing the struggles, despair, and ultimately, the resilience of the human spirit."

"I kept forgetting I wasn't reading a New York Times #1 Bestselling authors book."

"You have such a good way of painting a picture, it feels like I'm there when I'm reading."

"I cried, I laughed, all the emotions."

"This book is not just a narrative; it's a raw, visceral experience that explores the complexities of addiction and the horrors of her father's traumatic brain injury."

"I'm only on page 40 but so far your book is so well written and an inspiration."

"The resilience. The strength. The patience. The love. The best kind of people. The Nanson's. Proud of you Bethy."

"Your book has opened things up for me that definitely need attention and I've been putting off."

"I think it really shows the complexities and grey areas around addiction so well and how there is no right way to go about it."

"That's how powerful I feel your story is. I know it will make a huge impact for those experiencing similar situations."

"So well written!"

"I cried and laughed several times."

"There's no doubt in my mind that your book will be such a useful resource for others who are facing similar struggles. I am SO proud of you!"

"You do have a way of hiding behind a vail of a smile and a joke. It took courage and strength to write this book and I hope you're super proud of yourself. It's hard to be so transparent and vulnerable."

"I think you will have started many conversations within families that may not have ever been had without your book."

"I'm almost halfway through your book. I have cried three times."

"The trauma she has been forced to navigate throughout her life is profound and I am blown away at her ability to speak so eloquently about it all."

"I know this book is only the start for you. You're incredible Bethy, don't you ever forget that."

"A must-read for anyone seeking a profound understanding of the intricate relationship between trauma, addiction, and the indominable will to survive."

EMOTIONAL TORTURE

A Memoir of Addiction, Traumatic Brain Injury and Trauma

BETH NANSON

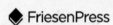 FriesenPress

One Printers Way
Altona, MB R0G 0B0
Canada

www.friesenpress.com

Copyright © 2024 by Beth Nanson
First Edition — 2023

ISBN
978-1-03-915364-6 (Hardcover)
978-1-03-915363-9 (Paperback)
978-1-03-915365-3 (eBook)

1. BIOGRAPHY & AUTOBIOGRAPHY, PERSONAL MEMOIRS

Distributed to the trade by The Ingram Book Company

TABLE OF CONTENTS

FROM CALM TO CHAOS

Up to the age of fourteen, I had a perfectly normal life. My alarm went off at the same time every morning. I got up, got dressed, got my sister up, ate breakfast, got my sister up again (her name is Katrina, Kat for short, and she was just simply not a morning person), and started gathering my things for school. By that time, Dad had already been at work for two hours. Mom was in the kitchen scrambling to make our lunches before she left for work for the day.

If Kat managed to make it out of bed, we would head to school for the day and see our friends. We attended Elphinstone Secondary School, a short drive from our house. After school, Mom picked us up and drove us to at least two activities: soccer, volleyball, baseball, basketball, piano lessons. It felt like they had signed us up for everything.

At six thirty, Dad came home off the ferry and Mom made dinner. We all ate as a family, then either watched *The Office* or a movie if it was movie night, or played a game if it was game night. Then we'd go to bed and repeat it all the next day.

My parents were happily married for thirty-something years; many of my friends' parents were divorced or divorcing so I admired their relationship a lot. Mom worked as a full-time community nurse, a job she felt lucky to love as much as she did. She was talked about highly, and everyone wanted her as their homecare nurse—that's how good she was at the job. She was located three minutes from home, an ideal situation to quickly dart home at lunch to let the dogs out to pee, turn the sprinklers off if she forgot in the morning—which was a common occurrence—and be home quickly after work to start dinner prep. She did all the grocery shopping, meal prep, and Costco hauls for the family. She organized all the gifts – anytime a family member got a present with a note stating 'From: The Nanson's', let's be honest, it was from mom. She was there for anything we needed: hair braiding, tickle scratches on my back, Halloween costumes, field-trip consent forms, you name it. She always reminded Kat and I that she was just one call away, that nothing we could tell her would scare her, that she wanted us to call her to get a ride from a party even if it was in the middle of the night. She created incredibly close relationships with both me and Kat. She was super-mom. She was well-loved by everyone, but especially by my group of friends. They all claimed she was the funniest, most entertaining, and most lovable mom they knew. As we got older, they all wanted to do the pre-party-drinks at my house so they could see my mom, too. They loved her, and I couldn't blame them.

Dad worked as a restoration biologist for the Department of Fisheries & Oceans (DFO); as kids the easiest way to explain his job was to say, "Dad saves fish", which is simply accurate. He also loved his job. And he was also well loved among the community. He taught Kat and I how to "toughen up" at a young age: riding our pedal bikes up our neighbourhood hills to Sprockids every Sunday morning, trying new sports and coming back stronger if we didn't make a team, continuing to be determined in any goals we had regardless of the number of times it took to achieve them.

We went on numerous family trips every year: Vernon or Manning Park for skiing in the winter, Hornby Island (where my mom actually grew up) in the spring, Point No Point resort for thanksgiving, to name a few.

Our birthday parties were raved about by our friends. Kat, having a summer birthday, was able to bring her friends out on the boat. My dad would take them tubing for hours while my mom organized all the food and activities post-water sports. For my birthday, in the fall, my dad would organize a large treasure hunt for my friends and I, while my mom took on the rest of what was needed for that special day.

Both my parents made good money, and we were privileged to have access to fresh, healthy food whenever we wanted. We had a beautiful home on the Sunshine Coast in Gibsons that my dad built with his own two hands. Our house had a forest in the backyard, and an ocean in the front. We lived close to the soccer field and our school. My dad coached our soccer team for many, many years, and my mom helped with a lot of the background organization for the teams. Mom organized carpools for the various activities we were involved in so we could still be home for dinner on time. My sister and I both had wonderful groups of friends. I guess what is of greatest importance to note is that we were privileged and happy. Genuinely happy.

It felt like we had a perfect life.

In 2010, when I was around fifteen, my sister and I started to become suspicious. Mom wasn't acting like herself. She was more careful to hide her belongings, in zip up purses and backpacks, keeping them close to her or hidden away where no one would find them. She would disappear into her room or the bathroom at odd times, for long periods of time. She went away for about a month, for some "work conference", but she had never been to one before. We started finding bottles of pills around the house and googling the uses of these medications.

When I say found, really what I mean is the stuff we intentionally searched for in her room; yes, invading her privacy, but I justified it by telling myself it was for a good cause. We were worried about her.

We were confused. Kat was a bit more equipped to understand what all this medical terminology meant. Not only was she older—and likely wiser—than me, but she was soon to embark on her post-secondary nursing degree.

I don't remember the details, but I do remember Kat and I talking to our dad about the things we had been finding. He agreed with our concerns and seemed puzzled himself. None of us knew what this meant, but we did know enough to know it was abnormal.

The problem? Addicts are damn good *liars*.

If we ever tried to ask her about pills, needles, or anything else we found, she would become defensive and lie:

"They are a patient's."

"Oh, those needles are just in case I get a stomach-ache and need a Gravol injection."

"That's not mine, it's a friend's."

"We got some extra supply that I haven't dropped off at the office yet."

Sometimes it actually made me jealous how *fast* she could come up with a story when she was on the spot. I can't get away with a lie if my life depended on it. Because of her lies, she was able to hide her addiction from the family for a long period of time.

I guess she had found her comfort in pain medication, Dilaudid to be specific. Dilaudid was the brand name for the drug Hydromorphone, a strong opioid. I wasn't sure at the time what she needed comfort from, but I grew to understand her tolerance to any guilt, pain or shame was low and something she wanted to numb. I can vividly remember when she told us. I guess the secrecy and lies were getting out of hand and with my dad constantly confronting her, she had no choice but to reveal the truth. Then dad decided we needed to sit down as a family and for us to hear it from her. I remember sitting in our living room; she said she had been sick, and that she was an addict. Those words really didn't mean anything to me; I really didn't know anything about addiction. I thought she was going to say she had cancer or a terminal diagnosis of some sort. I really didn't know how to feel. Was this a really bad sickness? Doesn't she just stop using and it's over? There was no plan at this time for further treatment. She didn't know enough to admit herself and we didn't know enough to push her to go. We all just assumed this would be a quick fix.

She was caught stealing drugs from work. This was a pretty serious offence, but considering she was clearly sick, her employer at Vancouver Coastal Health did pay for her to go to a thirty-day recovery centre in Toronto, Ontario. So off she went. I do remember her going away for some "nurse conference" around my grade ten years, and reflecting back, I now know this was when she went to Ontario for her first round of treatment.

I guess this was the real reason she was forced to tell my dad about her addiction; it would be somewhat hard to secretly get on a plane to Ontario for a month and hope no one you lived with would notice. My dad was willing to keep her secret while she was gone, to avoid worrying Kat and I, and because he probably figured she would be healed when she got back. It was upon her return that he had encouraged her to tell us.

As a nurse, drugs are easy access, right? Side note: my mom noticed over time that many people in recovery were doctors, nurse practitioners, nurses, and pharmacists because of this access. Mom was able to get her hands on anything she wanted, no one needed to know. Except, of course, the people close to her that started to notice the changes in her behavior: secrecy, hard-to-believe stories, random outings at odd times of the day, multiple bathroom trips, never going anywhere without her purse, limited ability to stay focused in a conversation, agitated, irritable, defensive. The list goes on.

The entire time she was gone, I was continuing to live life normally. Well, I missed her, but I knew it was just one month and I was still under the impression it was for a work conference.

This was the first time my dad was the sole parent in the house, and this shifted his regular duties. Suddenly, he was in charge of organizing carpool rides for our various sports practices, getting groceries, making dinner, and paying the bills. He always worked to pay for the bills, but Mom took over the act of actually paying them on time. I think there was a bit of shock as we all tried to make up for her numerous roles in the household. Dad was able to catch on fairly fast and I remember thinking he was doing a good job, even if spaghetti and smoothies were on the regular food rotation. Mom left big shoes to fill but he managed to fill them, nonetheless.

Mom's employer had saved her job for when she was back from Ontario, so returning to work was the next obvious step. I think the whole family was relieved that she was easily able to return to work. We felt this was a simple slip in life, and something from which she had completely recovered. Unfortunately, it was not so simple for her to slip back into a job where she was surrounded by temptation with easy access to her drug of choice.

Relapse. This was a new word for my vocabulary, but it wasn't long before I hated hearing it. Her dream job that she had worked her ass off to achieve was truly gone this time. Just like that. Only difference was that this time, the system was not so forgiving. Back to the recovery center. Back to our home without mom for the second time in 2010.

I could see the fear in my dad's eyes, but of course he would never admit to being afraid. I could feel the unease amongst the family. But I felt I had to stay positive for my own sense of hope, and for my dad, because I didn't want him to worry about Kat and I being thrown off in any way. He didn't need another concern at that time. I had to convince myself that Mom would get better, for good this time. She would get her job back. She would fight this. This would be the one and only relapse.

Little did I know that I was at the beginning of a journey that would go on for easily over a decade to come.

It took me a long time to understand how addiction works. I've always been a big believer in coming back stronger when you fall down, in giving life a push back when it pushes you, in determination coming out of loss or struggle. I love a good challenge. I am competitive. If someone tells me I can't, I will, and I'll do it better than you expected. So, needless to say, I had a pre-conceived notion that if my mom wanted her old life back bad enough, she could have it, and that was up to her. Her choice. Her decision. Her effort.

What I came to understand is that addiction is so much more complex than this. It's not something that has a quick fix. It is a grueling disease that takes over your mind and your body. It isn't something the addict decides to heal from one day; it takes immense effort and commitment to a recovery program to have any hope of sobriety. And that's assuming they are in a place, mentally, physically, and financially, to commit to recovery.

It's not just the addict that suffers; it's everyone around them too, especially when it comes to mental health.

I used to be extremely confident. I remember being fearless in high school. Well, I've always been a worrywart, but fearless in terms of not being bothered by what others thought. I vividly remember putting my hand up in class to answer questions, without giving a second thought to whether I was right or wrong.

I remember every conversation with anyone was easy: no pressure, no nerves, so simple. Of course, we all get nervous. I would feel the butterflies before sport games or tournaments, or before an interview. My dad would always tell me, "Nerves are good—it means you're ready." But I would never feel them for simple day-to-day situations.

I remember hearing of anxiety, that it's this thing people say they have that makes them worry a lot about silly things. I remember almost laughing when I would hear of people I knew saying they had it, because I just simply didn't think it existed. I have a lot of my dad's characteristics: "Walk it off", "You're fine", "Shake it off" and "Move on." So, it's not surprising that I would think people with anxiety just needed to "walk it off" and not be so dramatic.

I now realize I took advantage of having such high self-esteem in high school. I realize I was lucky and privileged to even think anxiety was a joke, because it really proved I hadn't experienced it in the slightest, and when it hit, I felt terrible for ever thinking it wasn't a real condition.

Mom came back from the recovery centre for a second time, and life went on. Well, not really at all the same as before, but it went on, nonetheless. We fought against her employer's decision to completely let her go, but the battle did not end well for us. I began to see how much more difficult life was for addicts.

It's no surprise that Mom would easily slip into depression, seeing as how her life changed from being on cloud nine to this. Her cloud nine was a version of herself and her life in which she could work, complete all the duties of a devoted wife and mother, and still use a strong narcotic drug. She was super-mom, but unlike before, her superpowers now seemed to depend on this drug.

It seemed odd that she would need a drug if she truly was living on cloud nine. This thought is what led me to believe she must have been struggling with pain for most of her life. She had Sjogren's syndrome, arthritis, and Raynaud's disease, in addition to depression. And maybe there was another mental health disorder that wasn't diagnosed.

Sjogren's is an autoimmune disorder in which your immune system attacks healthy tissues, often leading to uncomfortable symptoms such as dry eyes and dry mouth. Raynaud's is a condition which causes reduced blood flow to the extremities, usually in response to cold temperatures or stress. Arthritis, as most are aware, is an inflammatory condition that can often cause pain, stiffness and swelling in the joints. My guess at this time was that these conditions slowly got worse over time, and along with significant mental health struggles and easy access to powerful drugs, this led the way into severe narcotic addiction.

I felt bad for my mom. I loved her, and I knew this was a struggle. I felt bad that her life had been so viciously altered, which was not something she ever wanted.

I felt our relationship changing; I didn't want to add any stress to her life, so I avoided talking about hard things in mine. We were always close enough to tell each other anything, but again, I didn't want to burden her with more information that was only distracting from her sobriety. I knew whenever I asked her anything about her addiction, she remained defensive, which put more tension between us. I hoped this altered relationship would be short-lived.

An addict. How does one learn to manage their life with an addict so close to them? I don't know if I ever really learned how to correctly deal with it—is there a correct way? I don't know. All I know is the struggle of seeing someone you love so much not being able to choose the better path, not being able to envision a brighter future, not being who they used to be. Or have they always been addicts? Are people born addicts? Is it deep in the double-helical strands of your DNA? Or is it about your environment? The space around you, the influences left and right, the behaviors and lifestyles of people in your life. I know genetics can often lay the groundwork—it can load the gun—but it's often the environment that pulls the trigger. Was this environment traumatic? Was there a preceding undiagnosed mental health disorder that paved the path to addiction? Yes, I've done some research, and I'm confident in saying I don't really know specific answers to any of these inquiries; maybe it's a combination of all of them. What I do know is how an addict affected my life, for better, for worse, for a life that changed forever

ADDICTION – THE THICK OF IT

The chaos of everyday life with an addict continued, and despite my best efforts to convince myself otherwise, there just didn't seem to be an end in sight. It felt like I was walking through an overgrown forest without a clear beaten path; at first, I could see a way through to the other side, and it looked pretty close, a walkable distance. But as I continued trudging through the bushes, prickles started emerging, causing me to push past them with my bare hands. Vines started wrapping around my ankles forcing me to aggressively fall forward, the ground had turned into sinking sand, and somehow the distance to the other side had lengthened, so that I was barely able to see it anymore. Every time I considered turning back, in the hopes of avoiding more invasive bush whacking, another vine reached out and forcibly pulled me back in.

This is how I felt with my mother's addiction; I was trying to get to the other side with her where there was sobriety, and ultimately freedom. But the path there was excruciating and exhausting. And every time I tried to get out, I was ultimately sucked further and further back in.

What was I supposed to think when I came home from school, and she wasn't in a normal state? What if she was conducting some bizarre behavior? I saw these bizarre behaviors when I came home from high school, and I also saw them when I came home from university, whether it be reading break or summer holidays. I could be having a completely normal day and come home to her not in a normal state, causing a one-hundred-and-eighty-degree flip of my mental state. Bye relaxed, happy Beth, it was fun while it lasted!

What do I mean by bizarre behavior? What about all the times she was half asleep in front of the movie we were watching, and I wondered if it was really sleep or if she was so high she had lost consciousness.

What about the times she would forget the conversation we had five minutes ago and retell the same story again and again. I suppose this was a side effect of Suboxone, a medication she took daily to reduce her cravings for opioids, but it was bothersome that it came off like early Alzheimer's.

What about the time she crashed the car because "a bee was inside it" and distracted her. Was there really a bee? No one knows. The car was totaled.

What about when she was driving us home and I could see her eyes slowly closing in the rear-view mirror from the back seat. If I didn't notice and yell, would I be alive writing this book right now?

What about the time she somehow managed to message a couple of my friends odd texts late at night and didn't remember it in the morning. I checked, and memory loss does seem to be a common side effect of Suboxone, so I suppose this wasn't entirely her fault.

What about the time my sister heard a crash in her room in the middle of the night and walked in to find Mom on the ground holding her head, where she was aggressively bleeding from. She refused to go to the emergency room.

What about the times she has joked about suicide. That's not a damn joke.

I peed in the cup for her. Three times. I never thought I would be doing something like that in my teenage years. She was under supervision for a period of time, which basically meant they could call her at any point, and she had to immediately come in for a urine and drug screening test to ensure she was clean. This helped her chances of getting a job again. She needed to stay clean if she ever wanted a chance to work as a nurse again, which I know she wanted badly. But we all know by now that no matter how bad she may have *wanted* something, the addiction would take over.

She was mostly clean in this period, but I do remember a few times when they called and she had taken something the night before, which meant it was still in her system. She asked me for my urine. This made me sick. But there's not really any hesitation is there? It's *my mom*. I wasn't going to be the reason she didn't get a job again. She deserved a job again. She was in so much pain, she took a couple meds, and they happened to call her the next day. Imagine how hard it would have been for her to ask this—to put me in this position. So, it wasn't something for me to *think* about. I peed in the cup. She took it to the lab in her bra, went into the room, faked her own pee, and out she came handing them mine.

It's crazy the things you will do for the people you love.

These things sound brutal. They are. But don't forget who my mom was; don't forget she still had amazing characteristics. She still had days where I knew she was my mom and I saw the person I had always known and loved. She had days—even weeks—where she got back into swimming and gardening, made food all the time, was happy and upbeat with stories to tell and people to see. I still saw glimpses of the woman who lights up a room when she enters it. Again, when I see these sides of her, I have to take it because I don't know how long it's around for. I take it, but I also don't let it get me too excited, because I know this only means there's a *downfall* coming shortly, and the longer things are good, the closer that downfall is.

During that time, I wanted to be thankful that she was taking her Suboxone every day; it *should* have been the positive thing to look at. But it was difficult when there were a million other things wrong with the situation.

I could have had such an amazing relationship with her. I did have a good relationship with her, but it constantly made me wonder how much better it would have been without all the lies, suspicious behavior, and fights. It made me angry to think of how our relationship would have been without all this chaos. We would have been best friends. I mean, we were best friends. We used to tell each other everything, send each other funny memes, and laugh endlessly while making snap chats. I remember I would jump out of random places in the house to scare her, while filming it of course. We would rewatch them together so many times, both laughing so hard at her reaction. But it was only good for so long before there was a crash. I tried to take the good and pray the crash wouldn't be the devastating ending we had all been worried sick about.

Choose your battles. The thing I had been taught to do best with her. If she drank one night, would I worry? Well, drinking wasn't ever her main problem, but seemed like it could have been an issue on the side while getting through the tough times. So, was it something to bring up? I knew it would make her feel defensive, angry, and feeling like she's being watched all the time.

Back to feeling sorry for her. It must have been so hard being constantly watched, judged, and criticized. It was difficult to explain to her that it was only because we cared. I felt for her. I mean, if I got drunk one night, who the hell cared? But if she got drunk, it was all fingers pointed at her. It was people wondering if she should have done that. *What does it mean? Is this a problem? Should we be discussing it with her? Should we call a family intervention?* But all she wanted was a small break from reality and to have some drinks. So what?

The result is people talking about it as if it was a bad decision. That would be hard. I get that. But then why can't you be honest with everyone from the get-go, just make sure they know you might

13

drink occasionally but it's not a problem because you're not an alcoholic, right? It was still unclear to me at that time if drinking was an issue for her.

I had never seen my mom as emotional as she was after her first few relapses. She used to be so tough, like nothing could bite her. If there was gossip, rumors, rude people, *fuck* them. She didn't care. Nothing could knock her off her feet. But after these relapses, it was like she was suddenly crazy sensitive. If someone looked at her sideways, she'd end up in tears. I had never seen her cry so much, over things that she would have laughed at five years prior. Who was this person? This was not the mom I knew. I was confused. Was she high? Was she drunk? Was she really this upset? Was she just simply so embarrassed and upset with her past that she had become unbelievably emotional? Did I feel bad?

I wanted to shake her out of it. Who cares what anybody else thinks? Shake it off. Be honest. Move on. But man, that must be way easier said than done. So where do I stand? Do I push her to be better, to be more confident? Or do I stand by, watch, and sympathize with her? Is it a combination? All these questions constantly running through my head. I would be up worrying until midnight, when I had to be up for work five hours later.

This worrying never seemed to stop, from high school straight into university. I remember thinking about mom all the time.

I found it so unfair. I couldn't believe I was wrapped up in being so incredibly worried about my mom at age twenty-one. Weren't our parents supposed to be worried about us? I didn't want this on my shoulders. It was *heavy*. She was not the mom I knew. She was not the wife my dad married. And she was certainly not the woman many others used to know. It felt unfair that I had to worry so much, that I had to come home after working all day to see her high on something.

Of course, my mom provided for us for many years too, but it wasn't fair that my dad had to work his ass off to provide for this family while she was at home, too depressed to do anything productive. It wasn't fair that his work didn't seem to be appreciated by her. But again, it wasn't really her fault, was it?

I hated it when my dad got mad at her. I have always hated when my dad was mad, period. I value his opinion over anyone's; he's the biggest role model in my life by far. I feel like we're always on the same page with how we feel about Mom, or about anything.

But anger doesn't seem to solve anything. I worried about their marriage. I didn't see them separating simply because of the inconvenience. They were still our parents. They would still live together. They would both still love us. They would both still support and provide for us. So, what was the point? But I began to wonder if they really still loved each other.

I couldn't believe what my dad had put up with. And yes, I couldn't believe what my mom had gone through. But she wasn't the only one suffering; this was a family disease, it was all of us, but especially my dad. I give him credit for all that he has had to put up with. And I'm certain I don't even know the half of it because that's the type of person my dad is. He didn't want us to see more bad sides of Mom than we already had at this time.

It must have been so hard for him. This was his marriage, his wife, the woman he fell in love with, causing him pain. But he still looked out for her, still protected her dignity. What an incredible guy. What a selfless person. But did he still *love* her? Could he? Or, like I mentioned, was it just convenient at that point to stay together? Thinking of them staying together but not being in love was one of the biggest heartaches for me.

We got to the point where family dinners were dysfunctional. They would start off relatively normally, but Mom would often have a glass of wine with dinner. Because of her medication, she was more sensitive to the alcohol. She came off as drunk, disengaged, bored, and needing distraction. It was like having a toddler at the dinner table.

I would get so damned excited to talk to my sister and parents about life: my courses, varsity athletics at UBC, friends, funny things I had heard. I even made lists to remember what I wanted to tell them. I know, nerdy.

To me, sitting down with them was the best part of my week, and sometimes month. I looked across the table at my dad and sister and see their engagement; their eyes were locked on mine and listening to every word I said, asking questions, wanting to know more, wanting to be there living vicariously through the story I was telling. They were so engaged I swear they wouldn't have noticed if Steve Carell walked by our table.

I cannot explain how disheartening it was to look at my mom and get the opposite reaction. I know she didn't mean it, but she looked bored. She looked drunk. She looked like she needed a distraction, and that she would rather be anywhere else.

Ouch. It made me feel like she didn't care what was going on in my life. It made me feel frustrated that she wasn't listening; isn't this stuff you want to hear? Shouldn't you feel lucky that your kids actually *want* to see you, hang out with you, tell you everything about their lives? I can't tell you how many of my friends don't care to have a relationship with their parents at this age. And yet there I was, wanting so badly to have a relationship with my mom, and she could take it or leave it.

I'm sure this wasn't actually how she felt, and I know she would be heartbroken if she thought she ever came off like that. But then *why* did she do it? If you know your medication can't handle any alcohol on top of it, then *why* do you do it? So maybe alcohol was a problem after all? But she would never admit to that. She always refused to admit that she was semi-drunk at family dinners, even though we could all see it. It made me think I was crazy; is she drunk? Or is this a weird side-effect from her medication? Regardless, if she knew this was the outcome, why drink?

So, back to the usual train of thought: do I say something? I feel bad because we're finally all getting together, do I really want it to result in a fight? No. But what the hell is going on? I'm curious. I want answers. I want to know *why* she's doing this. I want to know if there are other things I'm unaware of right now. I want to know if she's able to simply just cut the drinking if she says it's honestly not a problem. I want to know if family dinners would change as a result. But what I really want is to have her be back to normal. I want her like she used to be: engaged, creative, full of life. I want normal family dinners like they used to be, when there was no drama, no judgment, no tears, just quality time. Is that too much to ask?

MIND GAMES

Despite the struggles at home, I managed to graduate high school in June 2012 and was accepted to the Food, Nutrition, and Health discipline at the University of British Columbia (UBC). My goal was to get into the Dietetics program one day.

Leaving home was bittersweet. I was excited to start this next chapter in my life, but I felt a sense of unknown for both my mother's future and my dad's sanity as he tried to navigate that alongside her. Although I had a wave of wondering if leaving was the wrong thing to do, my dad would never have allowed me to put a pause on my life for my mother's addiction; he still wanted me to live my life to the fullest that I could.

It was the fall of 2012 when I started my first year at UBC at seventeen years old. Not only was I a first-year university student, but I was up against the grueling UBC sciences. I stupidly took on many more courses and labs than my advisor had recommended, not sure why I felt I knew better than her. This was not really the most relaxing environment.

I didn't know how to deal with the problems at home. I was able to see how much it was affecting other areas of my life, especially my relationships. Being constantly distracted with Mom's health, her relapses, and the responsibility that fell on my dad was enough to make anyone crazy. This distraction led me to be unable to lend my attention to others. Instead of putting other people I loved first, I let them fall by the wayside because my brain didn't want more tasks to take on.

With the lack of control at home, I found myself in a desperate need to control something in my life, whether it be academics, sports, or jobs. Putting immense focus into these areas helped me feel in control, but only exacerbated the lack of prioritization I had for the people I loved. I didn't know how to cope, but I knew I needed to focus in school or I was going to fail.

When I was in first year, my mom was stable and at home, back to her daily routines. Not working of course, but getting things done around the house and still fighting to get her job back. I guess this was enough comfort to allow me to focus on school as best as I could.

My sister started receiving counselling in her first year of university and never regretted a second of it. She had been drilling the idea into my head ever since. But I didn't feel I needed any help because—well because, as you'll start to see, I'm stubborn like that. I felt, as many likely do before they embark on a path of therapy, that I was better than that, that I was stronger than that. I was worried that if I accepted help, I was accepting a title of weakness. Why am I so damn *stubborn*?

For four-plus years I refused help. I didn't need it. I was fine. I soon found out I did need it. I wasn't fine.

Throughout those years, I couldn't wrap my head around why Mom wasn't getting better, or why it wasn't a quick fix. I kept thinking to myself, *just stop using*, simple. I couldn't understand why she couldn't stop. She was human just like me and you, and we could stop things when we wanted, so why couldn't she? This was when I knew there was something fundamentally different about her brain chemistry. She would see her family struggling right in front of her eyes, but she continued to use. She would see that my sister had to start therapy just to cope with the addiction, but she kept using. She would see that I was barely able to keep up with the demands of my schooling, but she kept using. She would see my dad run off the little sleep she would allow him, but she kept using.

We told her over and over that we were so exhausted and falling apart, but she kept using. She would apologize for her wrongdoings and the pain she was causing, but she kept going. It felt like she didn't care enough to stop. I couldn't understand why she couldn't choose to stop.

Choice. I didn't yet understand that an addict doesn't choose; rather, they do. They can't choose. It's not a choice for them. My mom never chose drugs over her family, she never chose to lose her job, she didn't choose to have her family constantly worry about her. She didn't choose to hurt us. She didn't want any of this. But it happened anyways.

My dad tried to shield us from her addiction for a long time. He did everything in his power to protect us from more hurt. When he would fill us in on her latest relapse, he would intentionally leave the ugly details out. He would often have private conversations with her about her addiction so that we didn't have to constantly live with it like he did. He would always put on a brave face in front of us and act like everything was fine at home, when I knew it wasn't. He would always back us up when we would fight with her because he knew all too well that the addict was rarely in the right.

But as Kat and I grew up, we saw how much life he was losing being trapped in this addiction, and we demanded to be more involved so that the burden wasn't all on him. We became a team to see if we could beat this addiction. We came together for every relapse, every odd behavior, every disappearance, and made a plan together. We made sure to check in on each other and support each other in every way we could. We knew the language of addiction so well that explaining it to someone else almost felt foreign. We could finish each other's sentences, read each other's minds, and be on the exact same page for how to handle any situation with Mom. We were a solid team.

I continued inching closer to my degree, asking myself if I should have just become a doctor considering how much time I was spending in school. Although I wasn't home, I continued to fight with my mother.

Fights between my mom and I always followed a similar path. I would notice something about her lifestyle that bothered me. Now, I'll stop here to note that I'm not a judgmental person. The reason her choices bothered me so much is because they were self-destructive habits; things that would cut years off her life. Things that would shorten the time she would get to spend with me and with my future kids. So maybe I'm selfish for wanting her around longer, but I was angry she didn't act like she wanted it too. She always told me she did. But did she make choices that seemed like she did? No.

I would notice a habit that upset me—maybe it was smoking, narcotics, maybe it was behavior that indicated substance use, such as the inability to follow a conversation, displaying the "deer-in-the-headlights" look, smirking at inappropriate times, or sporadically crying. I would try to talk to her about these behaviors. She would become defensive and lie to me, as she had throughout my adolescent years. She would say they were my uncle's cigarettes, or she was at his shop and that's why she smelled like cigarettes, or the pills were a friend's. She was adamant that the alcohol I just pulled out of her purse wasn't hers.

I was so tired of the lying. I sometimes wondered if I would be less upset if she just told me the truth. Maybe. Maybe not. Hard to say. I would try to tell her I felt as though she was lying, and she would get more defensive and then suddenly it was a full-blown argument.

When my mom got defensive, she tended to say things she didn't mean. Hurtful things. Things that made me wonder if it was my mom talking or the drugs talking. Things that made my heart ache. Somehow, the tables always turned, and I felt like the bad guy while she was the victim. I was left wondering; *how did that happen? Why do I feel bad now?*

I began to realize that dealing with my mother's addiction was like a mind game.

It was a constant battle in my head—I felt so bad for her. She didn't want any of this. She was pained that she had affected the family and the ones that loved her. She needed to change. But could she? Did she have control over that? I felt bad. But then I was angry; angry at the dishonesty, at what looked like a lack of effort. Angry at the fights that arose within the family because of something she had done. But then I felt bad again; no one truly knew what she was going through inside, it must have been so hard. But I was still upset.

Fifth year came along. Yes, I know school took longer than it should have, which is a long story – could probably be another book. I was coming up to my twenty-second birthday. I should have been coming into that year excited, as I had heard I got accepted into the Dietetics program at UBC, something I had worked tirelessly for during the past few years —volunteering, getting experience in the field, reaching out to other Dietitians, touching up my resume and cover letter repeatedly.

But my mom and I had a fight right before I came back to school. I was so distracted by her chaos, so overwhelmed by it, so consumed by it, that I wasn't even motivated for things I really cared about. Despite getting into this wonderful program, and despite coming up to my twenty-second birthday, I had not one happy bone in my body. Instead, I thought about my mom constantly. I had never wanted to leave school, never felt the urge to be home, never not cared like this in my life before.

This was the turning point for me. After seven-plus years of refusing help, I was scared into it. I was terrified with my lack of motivation. That's not me. That's never the way I've been. It felt difficult to accept that I wasn't able to manage this on my own. I felt like a failure needing help with my own brain that I couldn't provide to myself. But that's just the stigma of mental health right there, isn't it?

I felt like I didn't want to tell anyone that I was going to therapy because I didn't want people to see me act weak; again, the stigma of mental health taking charge. I had made every excuse in the book for not going: the time I could be spending doing something productive, the resources that someone else could be using, the money to spend on just ranting to someone about my problems, the distance to get there. I would use anything. I would use anything until I realized I was just hurting myself by continuing to avoid it.

So, after years of my stubborn attitude, I realized the only way to avoid feeling so lost was to ask for help. That was the day I finally made the difficult decision to seek out counselling.

Luckily, I liked my counsellor out at UBC. I didn't have to go through introductory sessions with multiple counsellors until I found one that I liked. She was amazing. There was this feeling of safety in her office. I could tell her anything, and she had no bias, no judgment. She didn't know any of the people I was talking about. That helped.

My counsellor reminded me of a couple important concepts: acceptance and choosing your battles.

Acceptance. What is acceptance? How do I accept? I love my mom. I always will. But do I accept that this is her life now? She will always be an addict in some shape or form. She will relapse. Is that okay to me? Is that what acceptance is, being okay with it? I don't think so. I suppose acceptance is just realizing that this is a disease she has and being more understanding about what she is going through. Accepting that it will be a work in progress to get her healthy, and she may never be one hundred percent, but we will always work towards that. I have a hard time with acceptance.

Choose your battles. This is something my mom would always tell me when I was annoyed with someone. "Decide if this battle is worth fighting, Bethy", she would say.

Ironically, I found I had to do this a lot with her. She would have little awareness, for example, of when people were sleeping, and instead make noise left, right, and centre. But hey, she wasn't doing drugs, so was it worth getting annoyed at her? Was it worth the battle? Probably not.

She was, and is still today, constantly late for things, leaving with barely enough time to get places. This was especially frustrating when she was your ride. But hey, she wasn't not doing drugs, so was it worth the fight? Probably not.

I would see her smoking and it killed me inside as I figured it was just yet another way to cut years off her life, but hey, she wasn't doing hard drugs, so was it worth the fight? Probably not. I found I was constantly weighing things out in my head. I had to choose what was worth fighting about and forget the rest.

A few months after I started counselling, Mom had another relapse. She wasn't staying clean for any significant amount of time. This time, I was upset (go figure) but I was also numb. I didn't know how to feel when my sister told me. Was I angry? Upset? Annoyed? Sad? Feeling bad? All of them at the same time? I didn't know. I had never felt numb like that before. I wondered if I was just getting used to the chaos. Was that a bad thing? Was it acceptance? I wasn't sure. I didn't know if I should worry that I wasn't crying or angry.

Anxiety is always accompanied with one million questions.

It was a roller coaster. She had weeks—even months—of feeling good, of being "normal", of being the mom I knew and loved. And when I saw that person, I cherished her. I had to. I didn't know how long it would last so it made sense to just take it when I could get it.

Then, like the flick of a switch, something would happen. Maybe it was a relapse. Maybe it was neurological issues from different medications causing her to display some bizarre behavior. But whatever the driving force was behind the change, she was suddenly a mom I didn't know. A different person.

I remember it was hard to see her like that, but it was even harder to answer all the questions that were racing through my head. What happened? Why? How? When? Is there a solution? Is there an end? Do I support her and sympathize? Do I get angry? How do I feel? Is that the way I should be feeling? I loved when she was doing well, but it was also an uneasy feeling of wondering when the next downfall would be and what it would bring to this family.

Why had it happened again? Where had she gotten them? When had she gotten them? She had made a deliberate choice to take the drugs. She had purposely gone off her Suboxone medication to be able to feel the effects again of narcotics. So that's how much pain she was in.

Back to feeling bad. Her arthritis, Raynaud's and Sjogren's syndrome were so bad that her pain forced her to take the drugs, to ease the suffering, to feel numb. But isn't there anything you can do to limit the severity of these conditions? Simple things like moving around, heat and ice packs. Sometimes she chose not to do those things. Then my mind would tell me I'm annoyed that she wouldn't put in the effort to do this. But she was depressed. Depressed people can't really even think to do something, even if it will be beneficial for them. Then I would feel confused: was this true physical pain, or emotional? I would sit for hours pondering how to feel.

I felt scared that she consumed alcohol on Suboxone, something that can easily result is respiratory arrest and death. I was angry she wouldn't take every opportunity she had to get better. But I felt sad for her situation; I couldn't imagine going through what she was going through. Job loss, family suffering. Stuff she didn't really choose. I also judged myself a lot, too. *Am I being too hard on her? But it's for a good reason, I care about her and just want so badly for her to be healthy. But is it coming off like that?* I was starting to think that maybe I didn't understand this whole addiction thing well enough to even be speaking about it.

I sat. For hours. Thinking.

I felt as though I was stuck in the fight or flight sympathetic nervous system response. I could feel my cortisol constantly elevated, which was a key reason I was often feeling an increased heart rate. I felt bad for my body as I reflected on what was going on inside; my brain was on high alert for any potential danger and my ability to rationalize had gone out the window. My brain felt so preoccupied that there was no room for anything else. That combined with the constant distraction of my mother's addiction were key precursors to the cognitive deficit called brain fog, or as I like to call it, going blank.

Post-high school, the biggest change in terms of my mental health—that still affects me to this day—is that I go blank. I go blank, a lot. For no good reason, other than nerves. I remember myself in high school: the one that didn't get nervous for much, put up her hand all the time in class, didn't care what others thought. Yeah, that was short-lived. This brain fog thing was painfully real.

Because I was now a more anxious person, stemming from being so worried about my mom all the time, I tended to be nervous for things I was never nervous for before. In my UBC classes, I would know the answer to a question, but there was a debate in my head around putting my hand up: *what if it's wrong? What will happen then? Well, I'm like ninety-nine-point-nine percent sure it's right... is that sure enough? I don't know. What if I sound ridiculous? What if I go blank? I think I'm already going blank. Shit, I guess I better put my hand down. I already forget what I want to say.*

It was brutal, this train of thoughts going through my head during class. Sometimes I just started talking in class to answer something and somewhere along the way I thought to myself, as I was still talking, *where the hell am I going with this? What was the question anyway?* So sometimes I just made humor of it and told the class I didn't know where I was going with that comment. They laughed. I felt better. But I was still bothered by this change. Why did I get so nervous?

Sometimes it even happened when I was having a simple conversation with someone. Sometimes it happened when I was having a Zoom meeting with people I knew that would never normally make me anxious. I remember thinking, *I better get a hold of this or I'm going to lose my social connections, fast.*

This is what led me to experience the physical pain of anxiety, which was another aspect I didn't think existed. Often times, I would just be sitting in my room, at my desk, doing homework—well, distracted with thoughts of course, but *trying* to do homework. No one was around. My door was closed. No reason to be nervous. But I was.

I started feeling anxious and I stopped to ask myself why the hell I was feeling this way, what the *fuck* was I anxious about right then? Who knows. But I felt it, and I felt it right in my chest. BOOM. This heavy, uncomfortable ache; not so bad where I thought I was having a heart attack, but not simple enough to ignore. Breathing felt funny. It wasn't really hard or anything, but I noticed it felt different. It came and went, just as anxiety tends to. But it scared me.

Anxious thoughts, worrying about things I've never been worried about before, thinking the worst possible scenario for everything I do, being prepared for eight different possible ways a situation could go down, building things up in my head only to realize none of them happened in real life, fiddling with things more often—this is why I put rings on my fingers and starting jerking my knee—an inability to calm my mind down, finding myself with a sore jaw or neck by the end of the day, experiencing shakiness, sweating, or difficulty breathing for no apparent reason…

I had started unintentionally catastrophizing, which only proved my inability to separate real life from my anxious thoughts.

If the drain in the bathtub isn't draining properly, I picture the entire house flooding with water and I can see myself and my family desperately trying to escape. *The damn drain just needs to be de-clogged and all is well*, says my logical brain.

When I leave the house, I think, *did I turn the element off?* Even if I wasn't using it, my brain convinces me it could have gotten turned on somehow. I can picture the house up in flames and it forces me to turn around the car to double check. *Of course it's off, it was never on*, says my logical brain.

If it's windy outside, I picture a tree falling on our house and crushing it, along with those of us who are inside. I cringe at how painful this death would be. I think of where we would hide and how we could try to stay safe during this natural disaster. *It's just some wind, a normal type of weather*, says my logical brain.

If a cup drops on the kitchen floor, I am so startled that it takes more than a few minutes to slow my heart rate down again. *It was just a cup dropping off the counter, a very normal occurrence in life*, says my logical brain.

If I hear something outside at night, I am certain it's a serial killer with a gun who's going to come in and shoot me, and I play it out in my head wondering if they're just after me or if they're after my parents as well. Will it be a blood bath of three people or just one? What will the police say? *It's just a damn racoon*, says my logical brain.

If Kat texts me and says, "Can you call me", I am convinced she is going to tell me that mom passed away. I feel my chest getting tight and my breath getting short. *She probably just wants to catch-up and see when you're coming into town next*, says my logical brain.

Trauma always leaves a scar. The trauma of living in such an unstable environment left me with the scar of physical and emotional anxiety. Once again, I realized I was in over my head and needed help.

I had dropped counselling for a while, thinking I was cured after a session or two. I wonder how my brain convinced me of such ridiculous things. There was no telling how long it would take for me to feel better. With these emotions, there is no set timeline.

So, I decided to add more. I sucked it up and started going to group sessions on top of my bi-weekly one-on-one sessions at UBC. I almost didn't go to the first group session, thinking, *this is ridiculous. I don't need this. I'm fine.* I was nervous of who I might see there; *what if I see one of my teammates? What if I see the cute boy on the baseball team? I don't think he'll be so into dating me when he finds out I have a baggage of trauma that comes along for the ride. What if I see a professor and it changes the way they mark my work?* But then I thought to myself, *if you see them there that means they have decided they need this too, so you can't really just sit there judging each other.* That helped. So I went, and that's something I won't ever regret.

I'm glad I didn't take this opportunity away from myself. The group sessions reminded me that others experience anxiety too, and some to a much more severe extent than me. It made me feel grateful. It made me feel motivated. The room was a safe environment where there was no right or wrong, no judgment, no pressure, just learning.

I learned strategies to manage my stress and anxiety. I used the Calm app almost daily. At first, I could barely keep focus for even forty-five seconds, but I trusted that over time, my concentration would improve. I learned how to be mindful, how to forgive myself, take care of myself, love myself. Most of the strategies I vibed best with were humor-based; pretending I was a non-stop radio show: "This just in, Beth is freaking out again. She's not sure why, she usually isn't. See you next time on the dramatic life of Beth."

Laughing and making light of the situation has always been a coping mechanism for me.

I vividly remember trying to fight my mom for her keys while I was living at my grandmas in my later years of university. I wanted her keys so she wouldn't drive when she had been drinking or using drugs. If she wouldn't listen to me, I would threaten to call Dad. It wasn't funny at the time, but I laugh about it now—actually, we all do, including my mom, who used to threaten to call our dad when we misbehaved as kids. The tables had turned, and I was now the one threatening the phone call to Dad if the behaviour didn't change.

I have to create laughter and some lightheartedness where I can, where appropriate, because sometimes it's the only thing I have to hold onto.

I'm not healed. I don't think I ever will be anxiety-free, but I'm learning ways to manage it. I'm learning the areas I have control over and understanding to let go of the things I don't. This is difficult.

FROM NARCOTICS TO ALCOHOL

My mom had never in her life had an issue with alcohol, or at least not a serious, known issue. *Never.* But her narcotic addiction transitioned smoothly into an alcohol addiction.

After finally starting to take her Suboxone consistently, her desire for narcotics seemed to lessen. But she had to replace it with something, and she found a new kind of pain management by mixing Suboxone and alcohol.

This combination can kill you. She knew that. She played with it, still, because she's always loved playing with fire and pushing limits as far as she can. A risky personality trait to say the least.

The effect alcohol had on her was very different than that of the narcotics. Pretty much all the toxic behavior that came with narcotics was also present with alcoholism, but alcohol made her mean, really mean. The speed at which her behavior changed left me dumbstruck. She'd have a couple of great days, days where she would soberly tell us she's done with the booze, done with games and secrets, done with treating us like she did. It was convincing. I didn't know if she was upfront lying in these situations, or if she really did believe this and then had slips because she was so addicted. Probably the latter. Either way, it was convincing. I would feel hopeful. I would believe her. I believed she was done with the alcohol. I believed she hated the way she had treated us and what she had done to this family.

I believed she wanted to get better. Even when I thought she was bullshitting, I still chose to believe her because I wanted to so, so badly. That addict heart wanted a better future, but that addict brain strongly disagreed.

All the stories to come are a result of alcoholism, and the more I reflect back, the more convinced I am that I would take the narcotic addiction over the alcohol addiction any day.

I was entering my last year of schooling, my internship year. This was the year that dictated whether I would pass and become a successful dietitian or not. It was nerve-wracking to say the least, and it clearly didn't have my full attention. I was living at my grandma and grandpas—we called him Whooee, which is a long story, so I won't get into that—in North Vancouver.

They had a suite downstairs that I moved into just before the internship started. I felt lucky to live rent free but also to have been given the opportunity to spend more time with my grandparents and be of help to them as they got older. My dad also used it for the weekdays when he was working in town, so he didn't have to do the daily commute on the ferry from Gibsons. My mom technically lived with us down there too, but she was in and out of rehab a lot.

This was a tough year for her addiction. She was drinking pretty heavily most days of the week, and her sober stretches were becoming smaller and smaller. I wasn't sure what continued to drive her over the edge; we were all healthy and there wasn't any current trauma in her life, I didn't think. I suppose whatever mental health issues drove this addiction in the first place were not managed well up to this point. She needed to go back to the detox facility. Same old. The difference this time? I drove her there.

I picked her up and unfortunately, she had taken a bunch of something, because what addict wouldn't if they knew they had about eight hours until they go to the detox facility? It's like when someone wants to go on a diet and they say, "Okay I'm starting tomorrow, so I'm going to have all the fucking candy and chocolate my stomach can handle today!" I'm a non-diet dietitian anyways, but you get the point I'm making. She was messed up.

I tried asking her what she was so upset about. Silence. I tried asking her if she was concerned with her own health. Silence. Crying. I asked her if she knew something about her health that she wasn't telling us. Silence. More crying. Alright well fuck, that's one way to freak me right out.

It was always a relief when I dropped her off. I remember thinking the same thing every single time: *Okay, she made it there. Alive. She can get help now.* But the sadness settled in just as fast as the relief.

I'll never forget watching her walk up to the detox facility door. Still crying, dragging her bags behind her as she slumped up the stairs to the facility. The door was bolted and had a small window with metal bars on it. The outdoor walls were grey cement. It was dark out. It felt like I was dropping her off at a prison. She was still crying. I could see in her face and body language that she was utterly humiliated to be going back here and was terrified knowing that the first few days she was going to be walking into some really terrible withdrawals.

I've witnessed some withdrawal symptoms mom has displayed, but I know more about it from her responses when I've asked, and I'm sure that doesn't even do justice for the experience itself. She's told me about the nausea, the vomiting, the sweating, the tachycardia, the shakes, and the hallucinations. She feels sicker than anything she's ever experienced. She sweats so much it looks like she's just come back from a walk in the rain. Her heart races at a physically uncomfortable speed. She gets so shaky she can't write clearly with a pen on paper. She sees things that are not there, and only realizes when she watches her hand wrap around thin air instead of the imaginary object she thought she saw. One time she didn't recognize me.

I now understand that this image of her walking into detox is traumatizing for me. I remember feeling sick to my stomach watching her walk in; I will never shake that memory. I was so agitated that I pulled over and called my dad when I left. I bawled my eyes out. I didn't often cry. I didn't like crying. I especially didn't like crying in front of my dad. But I just lost my mind with how worried I was about her. Thank god I had him to help calm me down and be there for me when I needed it most.

Addicts typically spend about three to seven days in detox. Some will leave after detox and get back on track with their sobriety, and others will go straight from detox to a longer-term treatment facility for a matter of months. My mother usually required the full seven days in detox. She was back home in four days this particular time, and nothing had changed, you could see it right away. In the past, she had always come back happy, healthy, and back to her normal self. Back to my mom, even if she hadn't gone to long term treatment. She had never come back from detox like this.

Back to the drawing board. Back to trying to make her see that she's not healed, and she needs further help. It's like trying to teach a post-university student with a psychology degree how to do integral calculus. They didn't study it, so they don't know. But they are an adult, and you would think they could figure it out if they put in some effort.

Trying to get her to go anywhere for help was a battle. She would leave detox facilities before she had fully detoxed. She would leave treatment facilities within a couple days of arriving. She would leave hospitals within hours of getting a bed.

After this particular shortened detox stay, we attempted another location, something new: The Hope Centre. This was both an inpatient and outpatient facility that solely focused on mental health. We had hoped that we may get better results if we targeted the mental health issues first this time.

My sister had dropped her off. She was back within twelve hours claiming they didn't take her. Remember how addicts are chronic liars? There was no way they didn't take her after I had specifically told the nurse she was there for mental health, addiction, and suicidal ideations. She had left by choice. No facility can hold someone against their own will. I remember thinking that I wish there were exceptions for that. I wished that she would have a reason to go to prison, just to be kept sober somewhere and have a chance at a future.

I remember being shocked seeing her open the basement suite door to greet Kat and I as we came home that day, since we had expected her to be in the Hope Centre. My evening had quickly turned from studying to thinking of a plan B for her recovery. I remember following her around the suite like a lost puppy trying to get her to call detox, or Harbour Lights—another short-term recovery location—or Lion's Gate for other potential options, or anything. Just anything at that point. She had the nerve to tell me to back off because she was going to Costco.

COSTCO?! ARE YOU KIDDING ME? DO YOU REALLY FEEL THAT BULK FOODS ARE THE PRIORITY IN THIS MOMENT?! I was so frustrated I couldn't even form words. She needed help. *Now.* She just left one place against medical advice (AMA), and she needed to find another. I was struggling, trying to make phone calls and get her help, and she was telling me she was off to Costco. She shouldn't have even been fucking driving. I felt helpless. I remember thinking I was the one who now needed the help.

So, I told her I was going to get her parents involved, and that hit a nerve. She threatened me. I told her to agree to getting help that night. She didn't agree.

So off I went into the TV room where her parents were. They basically witnessed me crying and yelling at her at the same time. I think this was the moment Grandma and Whooee realized how serious the situation was. They are the most caring humans in the world, but I think they had yet to see some of this stuff firsthand. Because of their natural ability to give everyone a fair shot, and because they have such kind hearts, I think they figured that whatever was going on with Mom would pass. She would beat it, or she would get through it with unconditional love and compassion from us.

Unfortunately, if we just love her without setting boundaries, we watch her harm herself, we allow her to harm herself, and then we have that guilt on our chests for the rest of our lives. I'm yelling at her because I love her. I'm crying in her face because I love her. I hated for them that they had to see their daughter like this, but this was the true reality we were living. Buckle up guys, it's a hell of a ride.

Our next option was forcing her into treatment, skipping detox altogether and hoping the treatment center would take her regardless. The idea of forcing her into treatment ripped my heart apart. It felt like chasing a toddler around the house who's throwing their jacket off, kicking their shoes off, and running anywhere but the car where you need them to be. I've chased her to get her jacket on, barely able to get one arm in as she snatches it out of my hand and runs away. I've sat her down to get her shoes on, tying the laces as quickly as I can before she gets up again. I've run around the house shutting and locking doors before she can escape out of them, getting there just in time to slam it and end up between her and the door itself. And I've had to forcefully pull her into the car, do up her seatbelt, and shut the door before she pushes her way out.

One time I remember barely getting her in there, pushing her hands back, slamming the door, and locking the car from the outside. I remember putting my back against the closed door with her banging her fists against the window behind me. I remember just taking a massive deep breath. *Okay. She's in the car.*

Being physical at all is heartbreaking. I hate it. It's another thing I need to work through in therapy. I know I needed to get her help or she would have died, but I hate that I had to drag her out of the house. I need to forgive myself and understand I acted for the right reasons, but it's really tough to do this.

She was back again within a few days. It felt like we were stuck in quite the cycle.

It was only a matter of days later that I got the call from my sister, who was panicked and crying. I went to lower Lonsdale with one of my closest friends; we were studying to ensure we continued to pass each internship rotation. I remember feeling my mother wasn't in a great state that morning; she had a sharp attitude, which usually meant she was drinking. There was nothing I could do for her, and she didn't want me there, so I decided to go study.

As I was with my friend, my sister was texting saying she's heading over to North Vancouver because she feels like mom is relapsing. At this time, our plan of action was always to get her to detox then treatment, so my sister was going over to help start that process. I was waiting to hear from her, to see if I needed to dart out and go help as well. I had actually already parted ways with my friend because I got a gut feeling something wasn't right, and I had wanted to head back to Grandmas to check in.

That was when Kat called me. My gut never lies. She told me that Mom had locked herself in the basement, and there was no noise coming from her side of the door. I drove up Lonsdale as fast as I could.

Four cop cars. One ambulance. This was the scene outside my grandma's house as I approached.

Kat had busted the door open to get in. The paramedics and police were already inside. Mom was lying in the chair, completely out of her mind, having difficulty getting breaths in and out. She would have spurts of somewhat waking up and telling us all to fuck off, that we aren't needed, that this is ridiculous. Whooee was sitting beside her holding her hand, and I remember how much my heart hurt seeing him witness the really ugly parts of his daughter's addiction. He was reminding her to breathe every time she stopped; that was his job. Not something he should have ever had to do.

Seeing her in that state—barely able to speak, unable to walk, barely breathing—is permanently ingrained in my brain and I would do anything to remove that memory.

My mom had multiple suicide attempts over the years, but I never thought she truly wanted to die. When she was in the depths of a bad relapse, she did attempt suicide, but was always unsuccessful. Part of my brain thought she was near killing herself for attention, as her addict brain tended to do anything for attention, but a handful of those times she came undeniably close to actually ending her life.

This particular relapse in the basement suite did feel like a real attempt. She was only found because Kat went over to the house, and mom didn't know she was coming. Mom had closed all the blinds so no one in the yard would see her. She had put a chair up against the door wedged under the handle so no one could easily get in. She didn't tell anyone what she was doing. If we hadn't found her, I do believe she would have died that day. This was another failed suicide attempt.

Hope lost, again. She was convincing. But then she drank. This is what hurt. This is what made me feel defeated and hopeless. This is what I couldn't understand.

She was doing so well. We had thought she was almost a week sober, which was good for her. I couldn't understand why she did it this time. She had started meetings at Stepping Stones, an outpatient facility for those struggling with substance abuse and mental health issues, and had a plan. It included weekly treatment groups, meetings, trauma management groups, therapy sessions, medication treatments, treatment referrals, and more. We had just started to feel some relief, and then she drank.

It didn't take much for her to become completely intoxicated. That scared me because I knew what that meant: her liver was starting to function sub-optimally. And we knew from family experience how quickly things could go downhill once your liver was unhappy. We have had relatives lose their lives because of it. She had a bright future if she wanted it, but it had to be up to her to take it seriously.

She's mean when she drinks. She's defensive as hell. She will block our numbers, blame us for her drinking, threaten suicide all over again. She says things that would make her cry if she soberly knew she was saying these things to her kids, husband, sister, nieces, mom, dad. Things that make me mad. Things that make me sad. Things that make me want to scream at her for the unfairness in her words. Things that make me frustrated at the verbal manipulation she throws at us. Things that make me question if she really just said that. Things that make me pinch myself, hoping to god this is a bad dream. Things that make me go back to realizing this is the addict I'm talking to, not my mom.

And the next day, she doesn't remember a thing.

THE DISEASE OF ADDICTION

Addiction isn't something that's battled and won overnight. It takes hard work, patience, empathy, compassion, understanding, forgiveness even when you're still angry, and constantly feeling like you haven't done enough to help.

Let's talk science for a minute.

The dopamine and grey matter in her brain are wiped. *What?* Let me explain that. Dopamine is the hormone we make naturally in our bodies in response to pleasure or enjoyment; it's the "want more" hormone. If I score a goal in soccer, release of dopamine. If I have a crush on someone and they ask me out, release of dopamine. If I do well on a test, release of dopamine.

If an addict takes a drug, *MASSIVE* release of dopamine. The addict becomes dependent on this release. Their body says, "Hey, look how much dopamine we make daily while taking this drug, I guess we don't need to make any more ourselves!" Their bodies stop producing dopamine naturally, so dopamine receptors start disappearing on cell membranes.

This is generally a normal response in biology; we make lots of something, our bodies develop ways to take up less. And if our bodies make too little of something, we develop ways to take up more. It's all about equilibrium.

So, here's the kicker: what happens when the addict runs out of the drug? What happens when they try to get sober? Their body isn't making dopamine, receptors are limited, and now the only thing that was creating the dopamine—the drug—is out of the picture. No dopamine, no motivation.

We take for granted every day the dopamine we make to do normal daily activities: having conversations with others, going out to the store, making food for ourselves, etcetera. Can you imagine not having enough motivation to get out of bed? It's tempting to tell addicts to get up and do something, anything. That's like telling them to just simply have their cells produce more dopamine. Doesn't really make sense, does it?

Now for the grey matter. Grey matter sits in the prefrontal cortex of our brains and is responsible for behavior, thinking, reasoning, decision making, and memory. Studies have shown that addicts' brains have significantly less grey matter. And I wondered for so long *why* she made these crazy decisions, and *why* she was acting so bizarre. Well, it's because she physically didn't have the parts of her brain to control these things.

Again, something we take for granted every day; it's not that hard making a good decision when you have the part of your brain intact that is responsible for making good decisions. Duh. It's tempting to tell addicts to smarten up, stop being so irresponsible and unreasonable. That's like telling them to simply create more grey matter in that prefrontal cortex. Doesn't really make sense, does it?

It's a disease. And addiction needs to be treated like a disease. Addicts lose control over everything. The drug comes before everything.

A doctor at my work once told me that addiction is partly controlled by the amygdala part of the brain, which is the same location responsible for breathing. She said she always tells families of addicts to hold their breath and wait until they feel that NEED to release. She tells them that the panic they start to feel when they know they need more air, that feeling of desperation for something you can't live without, is the exact same feeling the addict has for the drug. Essentially, they feel they need the drug for survival, just like we need air for the same goal. It really stuck with me. I already knew how powerful addiction was, but to put it into perspective of something we need daily made it that much more real.

But remember, if we get upset with her, or push her too much, her response is self-harm: "Well wouldn't it just be easier if I were out of the picture." This response gets us to back off immediately. And it works every time. We have to back off. She knows this hits a *nerve* with everyone. Suicide is not a joke. I can't say that enough.

And I wonder why I don't sleep.

These situations are frustrating, hurtful. The words sting when she says them, but she doesn't even know she's saying them. Most of these situations go the same way; the irrational cycle of conversations, or lack thereof, are pretty predictable at this point. But there are a few I will never forget.

I will never forget when dad asked her why she did it this time, why she drank this time. And in her addict composure, she didn't say a word, but pointed her finger towards me.

I knew this wasn't her, but these kinds of actions were getting harder and harder to shake off. I knew it was nothing I should take personally—it was just the addict-brain talking—but how could I not? I couldn't help but wonder if the whole 'drunk words are sober thoughts' thing was real.

I know I haven't been easy on her in her addiction. I started out not understanding it, telling her to just stop and do better. I wasn't grasping the reality of the power of the disease. In fact, I wasn't grasping the disease at all. Dad and I would watch documentaries on stories of addiction to try to understand it more, to try to understand it like Kat did. Even when I did understand it, I had empathy and knew it wasn't her fault, but I was still hard on her to get help. I was constantly on her ass about making a structured plan for recovery. Obviously this wasn't my job, but that's the tricky part about addiction—if you don't do absolutely everything you can to force them to get better, you feel you haven't done enough. The guilt is overwhelming. So, I stood there and looked at her face with her finger pointed at me, and I wondered, *is this my mother talking, or the drugs talking?*

I will never forget the summer she didn't get off the couch.

She wasn't just taking a rest day or having a weekend off because she was tired from the week. This was severe depression on top of a severe addiction. It's hard to look at someone you love who looks lifeless. I remember wondering what the point was of living if this is what it looked like. I could have the best day out with my friends, or be hiking, or be out in the community, but coming home to her like this on the couch immediately shifted my mind to a negative, dark place.

I couldn't believe that I couldn't just shake it off and move on. But it felt like we had jumped ahead forty years and I was looking at her on her death bed. I looked at her and wondered if this was the last relapse, if she would get back on the horse tomorrow, or if she would even be with us tomorrow.

I pondered what I could do to help, but I'd already dragged her to detox and treatment enough times that it was no longer worth the fight.

I felt the wave of guilt as I stared at her and then walked into my room without a word. I wish I wasn't triggered seeing her like this, but I was learning I had no control over what I was triggered by. It felt like my body and mind snapped into a place of anger and resentment, mixed with sadness and devastation, without me choosing to be there. I felt powerless.

I will never forget the ease of calling 911. At one point, they knew my first name.

I used to feel scared to call 911. I felt like I should have notes written in front of me with what to say. I felt nervous about who was going to pick up. I worried about going blank or not being able to answer their questions. It always felt like such a big deal to call 911, like you better have a damn good reason to do it.

The first couple times were nerve-wracking, but it only got easier. Once I knew the questions they would ask, I always felt prepared. I didn't feel nervous at all anymore, but I felt like this wasn't a good thing. When you've called 911 enough that it's a casual conversation, that's a red flag that you're calling them too much. When you've called them enough that they know who you are and who you're calling about before you tell them, that's a red flag you're calling them too much. When you can rattle off the answers to all their questions in the right order before they've even asked them, that's a red flag that you're calling them too much. So yes, it got easier, but I don't think that was a good thing.

I will never forget the first time Mom said she just need to off herself, that we would be better off without her. Unfortunately, this became such a frequent threat that I became numb to it and lost count of the number of times she said it after that.

I started wondering why she said it so much. I do believe she's capable of it, but I don't fully believe she will do it. I think in the manipulation of the addict's brain, they will say anything to get your attention, to make you change your mind, to change your course of action, or to stop forcing help.

She said it so many times that it lost all meaning. But no matter how much I could convince myself that she wouldn't actually do it, I still knew there was a chance she would, so whenever the threat came up, she would have my attention and I would change my mind and course of action. She would always get me there.

One time she actually faked a cancer diagnosis just to get our attention. I was all wrapped up in what type it was, whether I would have to quit my job, how I would get her to chemotherapy appointments, what the prognosis would be… I was panicked until I got my head out of my ass long enough to realize it wasn't true… anything to pull us back in.

I will never forget the most well-known recovery centre in BC saying she's the most severe alcoholic they had ever seen.

This shocked me. Although you would think I couldn't be shocked more than I had been already, this caught me off guard. I knew her sickness was severe, I knew she struggled a lot, but I didn't realize the severity of her addiction compared to other addicts. I know every addict has their own story and I think every one of them is a significant, tragic one. But I just didn't know she was one of the most difficult cases they had ever had.

This really put things into perspective for me. I felt less crazy hearing them say they struggled to get her on track. I felt like less of a failure when they admitted this was an extremely challenging case for them, too. I finally felt like some people understood and saw a glimpse of what we dealt with day in and day out. I just felt understood, and felt our reality was finally justified and shared among other people.

I will never forget the time I was on the phone with Kat while she was desperately trying to get mom to the hospital. Mom had fallen, was bleeding from her head and was very intoxicated. She left my grandma's house without telling anyone where she was going. Kat got into her car to go looking for her as mom was in no state to be anywhere but a hospital. When Kat saw her stumbling down Lonsdale Avenue, she pulled over, but mom was resistant to getting in the car. I remember Kat telling me she felt so helpless in this moment that she just started yelling "Help! Help!" on the sidewalk. Luckily there was a nearby police officer who came to support.

I remember feeling sick for two reasons. Frist, I felt sick that this was the life mom was living at this time. What an awful thing to live through. And second, I felt sick for my sister that her only choice in that moment was to start screaming for help on a public street. How brutally traumatic.

I will never forget Dad telling me about his experience finding her at the bank. He had a feeling she wasn't doing well so he went to go talk with her while she was at treatment. He was going to convince her to stay. By the time he arrived, she wasn't there, and the staff were just as surprised at her absence as he was. *How did you lose her?* Dad said he left the facility, stood on the streets of new west, and looked out at the water with nothing but fear. As he walked towards the water anticipating what he might stumble upon, he passed a BMO bank. *Of course*, he thought, as he confidently walked through the doors to find mom sitting right there with the bank tellers. She was sweet-talking her way into getting new credit cards because she "lost hers" (nope – they are just being kept by professionals at the treatment facility). My Dad told the tellers she was an addict from the treatment house up the street and that if they give her money, they're basically killing her. Their jaws dropped. Mom stormed out. Dad ended up chasing her as she ran out the doors and through the mall. When he was telling me this story, he said he felt crazy: "I chased her through a mall, and I couldn't stop running after her because I was so scared that if I let her get to the SkyTrain station, she might jump off the rails, and that would be the last time I saw her."

I will never forget the look on her face when I finally needed to tell her I didn't want her in my life anymore.

You never think you're going to have to say that to a parent. I guess it was more the fact that I couldn't handle her anymore; I still wanted her in my life, but I couldn't cope. I didn't know how long I was supposed to put up with this kind of behavior without setting some boundaries, but it was long overdue, I knew that much. At least a boundary would help prevent me from throwing further anger at her, anger for something she isn't actively trying to hurt me with. You would think telling this to her face would be a simple task given how angry and resentful I had been. But it wasn't. In fact, it was the exact opposite: heart wrenching. She looked sad, hopeless, and genuinely upset when I told her this. She started panicking, saying she was trying, she was doing her best, she didn't want the relationship to be cut off. This made me cry on the inside, but I knew I had to hold strong for this boundary. Her emotions were convincing, and I did believe that she really was sorry, that she was overtaken by this addiction and didn't mean to hurt me.

I believe that because I know no addict planned this chaotic life for themselves. But the difficult part was that even on Mom's good days, her sober days, her days of energy, she didn't take action to better her recovery. Her meetings were still half-assed, she wasn't working the steps, she wasn't taking on the role of being a sponsor herself, she didn't call her own sponsor enough, she wasn't doing community service, and she wasn't consistently taking her antidepressant. The small things that are part of a successful recovery are incredibly important in keeping you sober, but I didn't see them being done well. But maybe she was just that sick—too sick to do them well, and too sick to not be in denial about how poorly she was doing.

How do I win here? I needed to hold strong boundaries. I felt I needed to push her and make her uncomfortable so that maybe she would see that we weren't willing to put up with this anymore and she needed help NOW. There had still been relapses in the past when there were no boundaries in place, so I wasn't convinced their implementation necessarily triggered a relapse, nor that their absence prevented one. I felt a need to trust that my tough love approach may actually be helping her if it was the only way to get her to treatment. The tough love approach and the boundaries did seem to help lead to more sober time.

But hurting her when she's already down, telling her there's more to lose when she's already struggling—that was nearly impossible to feel good about. It was a lose-lose situation. If I said nothing, nothing would change, and I would get sucked into believing this is over and over and over again. If I said something, maybe there was a chance at treatment, but I was also putting her through incredible pain. How the hell are you supposed to choose between potential recovery and being the cause of immense suffering?

I will never forget sitting in the ferry lineup taking her to treatment and looking at her in the rear-view mirror: body hunched over, eyes closed, and drooling. My heart breaks with these images. *This can't be happening.*

I will never forget walking into the house during a particularly bad relapse and having a complete side-by-side visualization of her sobriety versus her lack thereof. I walked into the bedroom and looked to my left to see her passed out, the empty bottle of vodka on the floor by her right hand. This broke me. But what broke me more was looking to the right of the room and seeing the puzzle she had started on the table, the stocking she had started to fill, the gift bag she had created. These were all selfless innocent projects she was working on just prior to that first drink. This was her thinking about everyone but herself prior to that first drink. To the right: glimpses of the most wonderful thoughtful woman on earth. To the left: this wonderful thoughtful woman clouded by this ugly disease.

I will never forget the time I picked her up from detox and a patient asked if she was my mother. When I responded yes, he replied: "That's so cool. She's our mom when she's here, too." Goosebumps went down my spine as I could easily picture her taking care of her fellow addicts here, a characteristic she came by naturally. As I watched her put on her backpack and shoes by the door, I thought *please keep this sobriety so you can be my mom again, too. I want my mom back.*

I will never forget the countless times I found myself thinking of the speech I would make at her funeral. I guess it felt like that day could be right around the corner, and my anxiety brain felt a need to prepare.

I would catch myself subconsciously reciting the words I would use and stories I would tell. I would ponder whether I would discuss her addiction or not. I've always felt a need to talk about it, so that her actions and behaviors are understood and not judged.

I would think of the order in which I would say things. I would cry when I recited it because I knew I would be holding back tears the day of, standing in front of a large audience of familiar faces. I would get so taken over by these thoughts I would actually jump at the sight or sound of someone walking in the room because I had forgotten where I was. I forgot that this was something my brain was making up and that it wasn't real—*yet*.

I will never forget when my dad looked at her and said, "I just want my wife back." Ouch. My heart.

My heart broke hearing him say that. He deserves nothing but the best after everything he has been through and put up with, silently, without the slightest complaint. He has always put her before his own needs and continues to, regardless of her behavior. He's lost hours upon hours of sleep watching over her, like physically watching her sleep to ensure she is still alive. He forgives her over and over. He forgives her when he's trying to help her and her only response, while using, is, "you fucking asshole."

He forgives her *every single time*. He works with her to try and find more realistic solutions to better her health. He continues to believe her, no matter how many times the trust has been broken. He still loses his temper at times, but he has learned and practiced how to be utterly and painfully patient with her. He has, for lack of better terminology, given his life to her. And all he wants is his wife, he wants the woman he married. It doesn't seem like much to ask. Again, *ouch*. My heart.

I will never forget all the times I told myself under my breath, "She's not my mom right now, she's the addict. My mom would never treat us like this. An addict would."

This was coping, in a nutshell. You cope by telling yourself it's not her, it's a different person. And it's not a lie. She is a different person when she's using, all addicts are. As I've said before, addicts are wonderful people who have been stuck in a self-destructive disease and are barely clinging to life as they battle the power of this disease. It does help to remember she isn't herself when she's using, that the words she says and the things she does are completely foreign to us.

Reminding ourselves of this constantly is also a way to reduce resentment when she is sober. She is so sorry when she is sober, she hates what she has done. She genuinely feels horrible. So, if I remind myself that she was a different person when she was using, I can try to enjoy the real her when she is around.

I can't explain to you the constant fear I feel. I wake up early in the morning, or in the middle of the night, and my heart races as I open my bedroom door because I don't know what I'm going to see on the other side. *Will she be there? Will she be intoxicated? Will she be lying on the floor somewhere? Will the door be left wide open, and her shoes gone? What did I miss while I slept? Am I going to see something that will require calling 911? Better have it open on my phone just in case.*

I dial 911 without pressing that green call button yet as I cringe around every corner, trying to prepare myself for what I might see. My heart pounds through my chest. My brain shows me images of her body in a pool of blood, and I can't tell if that's something I'm about to stumble upon or not. I think of my action steps if I do run into her on the floor. I go to whatever room she's "sleeping" in and put my ear up to the door.

Do I hear breathing? The most important—and yet most daunting—question I ask myself. I wish for no one, not even my worst enemy, to have to ask themselves this question on such a frequent basis. As I silently hold my breath with my ear against the door, I pray to God I hear breathing. And if I do, I take a sigh of relief as I calm myself until the next "check." I'm twenty-three years old, and instead of going out to the bar on a Friday night, I'm just here making sure my mom is still breathing. There's something utterly wrong with that sentence.

When she's sober, she says she's sorry for everything she has put us through. I can hear the genuine tone in her voice, but I truly don't think she knows the half of it. She says she does. But she has no idea how awful this has been for us. Does she know what it's like to not sleep from stress or worry? Does she know what it's like to monitor someone twenty-four/seven? And no, it's not like having kids; kids don't threaten suicide, kids don't constantly play with risky habits that can kill them.

Does she know what it's like to worry to the point of experiencing physical symptoms? Does she know talking about her and figuring out plans for her now consumed our lives? Does she know Kat and Dad are taking time off work to deal with her? Does she know I am struggling with my dietetic internship, not sure I will be able to make it through? Does she know what it's like to try to balance her addiction with a life? How the hell do you balance addiction with life?

She has no memory of her worst moments, but they sit with us forever. And if we ever attempted to describe these moments to her, she would sit in denial and threaten suicide. We were always cornered with these tough decisions. How did she get so much damn *power*.

You never expect your parent to treat you like this. We're taught from a young age that even if you get bullied in school, even if you don't have friends, even if people don't like you as much as you'd hoped, it's okay because you always have your family. They will always have your back. You always have your mom.

It hurts me to say that I really don't feel I *have* her; I barley have her to talk to let alone work out my day-to-day stresses with. And it hurts me even more to say that my mom actually feels like the bully. The addict in her doesn't care to hear anything outside herself, and even if she did, she doesn't have the capacity to sit and listen anymore. She's on autopilot and she doesn't even realize it. But if I try to tell her that now, she'll just go back to her suicide threat, which will of course shut me up, so I guess that's out.

Addiction really is a nasty disease.

I don't think she realizes how damaged our relationship is. I understand she's an addict. I will *never* blame her for that. What I don't accept is the constant lying and manipulation, the denial of how bad this situation really is. She doesn't see the worst of it. But maybe I need to accept that these behaviors just simply tag alongside addiction, part of the disease rather than a deliberate choice.

I have no trust. I have a lot of resentment around how we've been treated by her. I have gotten to the point where I fear her. I used to fear a burglar or murderer coming into the house at night, but that fear is miniscule compared to the fear of seeing my mom up in the middle of the night.

I don't know her. And she may feel this is *dramatic,* but again, we are looking at this through two very different lenses. I do believe this is repairable. But it will take *years* of re-building connection and trust. I am willing to work on that if she is.

I have gotten in the habit of locking my bedroom door at night. *Fuck. I should go back to counselling.*

I got to the point where I didn't know what path to choose. I didn't know the right decision. I was beyond hurt and confused from trying to put together the pieces so that they made sense. I'm a logical person. I needed this to makes sense. But no part of it made any sense at all. Dad stopped staying overnight at grandmas, trying to evoke a response as this would lead to her not seeing him as much, and as a result, her kids didn't see their dad as much. Dad was talking about leaving his job to look out for her more. My sister and I were struggling to focus, to sleep. No one was sleeping. What is sleep?

Her parents became worried sick to the point where they could have serious health consequences as a result. Yet she didn't see the problem. She couldn't make the decision to just simply get some help after seeing her family struggle.

All we asked for was a plan. It could have been as simple as going to psychiatry appointments once a week, or going to Harbour Lights once a month, or getting a counsellor to see twice a week, or having a plan of attending two Narcotics Anonymous/Alcoholics Anonymous meetings per day. Anything that shows an ounce of effort for her health. *Anything.*

Her family was struggling, and she wouldn't make a plan. That's what I couldn't understand. No matter how many hours, days, weeks, months, years I put into trying to understand that, I couldn't. And that's the worst part of dealing with an addict. This is how they work. She wasn't being my mom, she was being an addict. My mom would never treat her family like that. An addict would.

My migraines got significantly worse. I've had chronic migraines since I was young, and there are various triggers such as dehydration, not eating enough, too much added sugar, exercise in the heat, high elevations, the list goes on. But stress is one of the bigger ones.

When I feel a migraine coming on, I have a short window to take the Advil, and if I miss it, I'm in for a ride. The pain makes me want to knock myself out; I hate needles, but I would take a thousand of them to numb me. I require a dark room and total silence. I can't find a comfortable position on the pillow for my head. The nausea kicks in and that's when I have to vomit. Sometimes throwing up makes me feel better. The pain is some of the worst physical pain I've ever felt in my life. My sister says I need to go to the ER when this occurs, but I can't even move off the bed to get there. My mom used to bring me cold cloths and rub my head until I fell asleep. I miss this so much.

These migraines have become more frequent, and more severe, over the years. I know most of them are a result of tension. I need ways to cope to move away from this result of stress.

These things don't just go away. They aren't just forgotten. In fact, it's the exact opposite; they are with you no matter how much you try to forget them. And that's what drains us, that's what makes us so damn tired.

I was tired of trying to separate my mom from the addict; it's difficult when both people are in the same body.

I was tired of waking up in the night to check if my mom was breathing.

I was tired of seeing my dad get up in the morning for work and feel for her pulse before leaving for the ferry. That wasn't the marriage he signed up for.

I was tired of hearing about her sleepless nights, the night terrors, the hallucinations.

I was tired of looking at her trying to figure out if she was currently in a different place, or in the moment with me.

I was tired of searching the house for drugs and alcohol and finding them in the most unimaginable places. I got into the habit of checking under my bed before I went to sleep, and in the piano after each weekend.

I was tired of us creating a babysitting schedule for her so that she was never alone. And I was tired of the unnecessary guilt of stepping outside of that schedule. If I wanted to go out for dinner, or if Kat wanted to see a friend, or if Dad wanted to get together with the guys, and it was our turn with mom, we couldn't go with the feeling that a relapse that day was on us.

I was tired of walking into the room after not having her respond to my verbal calls, seeing her laying there, and shaking her to get her out of the deep sleep she was in, terrified I was shaking a corpse.

I was tired of her aggressive behavior when she was using, how she backed me into a wall with her fists in my face because I had her keys and purse in my hands. It's not a nice image looking your mom in the eyes and feeling like she wants to hurt you. I didn't think she ever would, but it was still terrifying because I was also aware that she was not in her right mind in these moments. I had her keys and purse because I didn't want her to drive. I didn't want her to drive because I didn't want her or the public at risk, and because I didn't want her to get more alcohol. I didn't want her to die so I was desperately trying to take anything away that could lead her there. Her drinking and driving could kill someone, maybe it already had.

I was tired of the ambulance calls, and the ER visits in the middle of the night.

I was tired of calling a missing persons police search on her when she hadn't responded in seven hours. We typically knew she was drinking, and I was always ninety-nine-point-nine percent sure they would find her dead. The silence waiting for these calls weighed heavily. I can't explain the fear in my heart when the cops would call me back and my stomach would sink to my feet thinking about them telling me of her passing, that she was in a ditch, that she was unresponsive. That sinking feeling is indescribable.

Turns out she was found drinking alcohol and the power-steering fluid in her vehicle; another suicide attempt.

I was tired of waking up to Whooee yelling, "She's gone!" at one a.m. This was what made me not want to fall asleep, because I was scared of waking up to a real-life nightmare.

I was tired of searching the yard for her with flashlights in the middle of the night, scared I was going to trip over her unconscious body.

I was tired of the heart-wrenching protocol when I did find her: lifting her lifeless body into my arms to take her back to bed.

I was tired of seeing yet another drunk injury; last time it was broken ribs, this time she fell on concrete, smashing her face and breaking a finger. She looked beat up.

I was tired of the countless family interventions we were having; sitting in the living room, with each of us giving our endless reasons of why she needed treatment, and her throwing back denial and options that were less than useful in keeping her sober. These discussions would go on so long, often times the entire day would get away on us and I would sit there at dinner, completed exhausted, wondering if this would ever change. I'm not only exhausted that day, but for days after. I wake up the morning after these interventions and I feel hungover. It used to surprise me as I would remind myself it couldn't be a true hangover if I didn't drink any alcohol the night before. Now I just expect the symptoms: the headache, drained mind, and total-body lethargy from the mental marathon the day before.

I was tired of all my time and energy being sucked into this addiction. I constantly cancelled weekday or weekend plans to go rescue her.

I was tired of not being able to take a break while knowing how desperately I needed one.

I was tired of trying to explain to friends why I didn't have the energy to go out.

I was tired of feeling we were getting somewhere in our conversations, like I was close to having her agree to treatment after six hours, all for her just to quickly give me the middle finger before turning to walk out the door. *I guess that's a no.*

I was tired of using alcohol as bait to get her to detox, treatment, or just out of the house and away from dad. I would take the 2-6 from her, and she would be so fixated on it, she would do anything. I remember saying "if you want this, you need to put your socks and shoes on, and get into the car." She would usually comply. Anything for that drug. I was tired of feeling sick to my stomach for using alcohol in this disgusting way to get her closer to help.

I was tired of helping her get dressed because she was too inebriated to do it herself.

I was tired of getting hopeful when she finally agreed to go to treatment, only to be devastated when I heard she was leaving AMA within the first week. We almost had a week off, and this time I told her there was no family to come home to if she left treatment—that was her last chance—but she left anyways. I was tired of that kind of heartbreak.

I was tired of her missing birthdays, special events, and Christmases.

I was tired of utilizing the car rides to family events for discussing our story for mom's absence this time. Dad, Kat, and I would have to ensure we were all going to say the same thing when anyone at the event asked where she was. Usually it was a flare of her arthritis or Sjogren's syndrome, preventing her from joining. I was tired of hearing dad give the same excuses when the rugby or soccer guys would ask where she's been. They joked about him locking her up, and he would laugh with them while shaking his head, but I could tell he was thinking *trust me, if I could lock her up, it would be in treatment, and hopefully I would see my wife again upon discharge.* Her absence was noticed, and the excuses for it were becoming old. I was tired of constantly lying to everyone.

I was tired of going to school and pretending I was totally fine when I couldn't stop thinking about whether she'd be alive when I got home that day.

I was tired of the migraines.

I was tired of being twenty-five and feeling like I was living through having the worst teenage daughter in the world, who was my mom—the irony was painful.

I was tired of being on edge walking around every corner in the house, unsure of what I would see; hoping for the best but preparing for the worst.

I was tired of the hurtful words she said when she was out of her mind. I hated hearing her say, "fuck off" or "I can't stand to hear the sound of your voice." *You're* frustrated with *us?!*

I was tired of questioning if a fatal overdose was the only way out, and I was tired of beating myself up for even having the thought that that life would be easier at that point.

I was tired of anxiety—or more correctly from a medical stand-point, chronically high cortisol levels—and I was tired of obsessing over what this would do to my health in the future.

I was tired of living scared.

I was tired of *being tired.*

NARCOTICS ANONYMOUS

Narcotics Anonymous (NA). This is where it's at. This is recovery. It felt like this is what we had been searching for, and it wasn't until 2018 that we found it.

NA is a non-profit organization whose goal is to help those struggling with substance abuse to find long-term sobriety. They use a twelve-step program, similar to Alcoholics Anonymous (AA), with members being guided by a sponsor who is further ahead in their sobriety.

I don't fully remember how Mom ended up in NA, but I believe she was told every time she was in treatment to start attending meetings and had ignored that advice for a long time. It didn't take long for her to see the benefit once she started.

This space was different than anything she had tried before. Detox and treatment have their place in recovery, and are needed no doubt, but NA is where addicts can develop the strategies to maintain long-term recovery from substance abuse. There's a feeling of community, each addict having an overwhelming awareness that they aren't alone in their addiction, that there are others like them. They would recite readings from recovery literature, speak about certain steps in the twelve-step program, and share stories about their past and how they found recovery.

This is what my mom needed; a safe space where there was no judgement, where you can share your past knowing full well others in the room have done the same in theirs, if not worse. She needed connections with other humans, humans that were working a recovery program and could have a good influence on her. She needed more social outings, even if that meant going to meetings with other addicts. She needed a sense of belonging and purpose, and that is what this program provided to her.

She worked the steps and attended meetings as recommended by her sponsor. She was really starting to turn a corner in her recovery, for the better. I could start to see glimpses of her old self, especially when she would come home from a meeting. It was as if the meeting had completely changed her mood, her thoughts, her demeanor, and her whole perspective on life. She came home a different person, but a person we all remembered from the past.

I had heard the steps voiced out loud so many times I was starting to remember them:

1. *We admitted that we were powerless over our addiction, that our lives had become unmanageable.*

2. *We came to believe that a power greater than ourselves could restore us to sanity.*

3. *We made a decision to turn our will and our lives over to the care of God as we understood him.*

4. *We made a searching and fearless moral inventory of ourselves.*

5. *We admitted to God, to ourselves, and to another human being the exact nature of our wrongs.*

6. *We were entirely ready to have God remove all these defects of character.*

7. *We humbly asked him to remove our shortcomings.*

8. *We made a list of all persons we had harmed and became willing to make amends to them all.*

9.   *We made direct amends to such people wherever possible, except when to do so would injure them or others.*

10. *We continued to take personal inventory and when we were wrong promptly admitted it.*

11. *We sought through prayer and meditation to improve our conscious contact with God as we understood him, praying only for knowledge of his will for us and the power to carry that out.*

12. *Having had a spiritual awakening as a result of these steps, we tried to carry this message to addicts, and to practice these principles in all our affairs.*

We all benefited from NA. The whole family was uplifted knowing she may have found the answer, the key to success in overcoming an addiction. I felt a sense of relief knowing we had found something that might actually work. Something that might save my mother's life and bring her back to me, the way I once knew her.

I would go to some of these meetings with her, to show my support. Dad would often attend too, and Kat if she was off work on time. No matter how much hurt I had experienced, I knew that if I didn't support her when she did something really positive for her recovery, she may not feel as motivated to stick with it.

To my surprise, I found the meetings fascinating. I was inspired to see these addicts get together, tell stories and celebrate days, months, or years of recovery. I would hear other people's stories, how they managed to find long-term sobriety after years of sickness, betrayal, dishonesty, manipulation, heartbreak, pain, and grief. They would talk about everything they had lost in their addiction, and how ashamed they felt for the way they treated those around them while in the depths of their sickness. It was engaging listening to their reflections.

This one guy talked about the drug being everything; he lost his house, he fed his kids packaged Kraft Dinner with the money he had left over *after* he had bought his drugs. He then lost his kids. He saw his drug dealer driving his car, and his wife walking down the road with another man.

But this is what addiction does to you; you lose everything. And there he stood, years sober, because of NA. People changed there; men were vulnerable in that room, and it was wonderful to watch.

This one guy said, and I quote: "This program really works. I went from robbing drug dealers to taking pictures of flowers." I will never forget how hard I laughed hearing that, but also how inspired I was by this man I'd never met. I remember hearing a woman in tears stating that she'd just relapsed and lost her family again. She felt like no one loved her. Another man spoke up and said, "Well, we love you. Heck, I love you and I've never even met you. Until things get resolved with your family, you have us, and this is the space you can be in to keep motivated to push through."

I was speechless at the generosity of one addict to another. They look out for each other. When they are sober and working the steps, they carry characteristics we should all try to mirror.

I even caught myself saying the serenity prayer with them:

God grant me the serenity to accept the things I cannot change, the courage to change the things I can, and the wisdom to know the difference.

I know this is helpful for addicts to be reminded of daily. But I found it also helped me, because I too needed to accept things I couldn't change with this disease.

The group of people in these rooms were addicts, but they were wonderful, wonderful people. They made mistakes, had a rough life, and went through more shit than most people have, but at NA they were putting in the work to become better, and the results were astounding.

There's just something about feeling accepted, something about knowing you aren't alone in this and that so many other people struggle with addiction too. I think that's what my mom really needed for her recovery journey: to not feel alone, to feel accepted, to not feel shame, guilt, or embarrassment, but to feel pride in the steps she was taking, among all those other people, to recovery.

It's recovery until you experience something un-recoverable. I thought the worst pain of my life was behind me; little did I know, it was yet to come.

THE ACCIDENT

It was in the afternoon on Sunday, October 6th, 2019, when I got a call from Mom saying Dad had been in an "accident." Knowing he was playing soccer that morning, I asked the typical questions: "What is it this time—another pulled hamstring? Broken rib? Bulged disk in the back again? Maybe a concussion at the worst?"

It wasn't until she said he was having trouble breathing that I realized the severity of the situation. I think I had a mini stroke. I felt all the blood rush to my face, and I was struggling to figure out what to ask next. I panicked. And I mean like, I fucking panicked.

She said he was being air lifted to Vancouver General Hospital (VGH), so I got in the car faster than I ever have in my life and drove like a maniac to meet him there. I think I went through three red lights, and I know I was going at least twenty kilometers over the speed limit. People don't get air lifted unless it's a life-or-death situation, so that scared the living shit out of me. Kat met me there too, and so did Mom along with her sister and niece; they were escorted from the ferry by the police. Dad's sister, Patti, and her daughter got on the last ferry as soon as they found out and arrived in the ER that night.

I can see it so vividly, waiting in the VGH emergency. Seeing the sliding doors of the trauma bay open and close every time a doctor came in or went out. Every time the doors slid open, I scanned every stretcher that went by, waiting to see him get brought in. I knew it had to be soon. I was getting so impatient waiting for him, and then I panicked to finally see the image of him unconscious and intubated, an image I never thought I'd see in my entire life.

I could feel my body slowly slipping into total shock.

I can remember the chaos of doctors talking, surgeons coming in and out, nurses adjusting different lines and meds. It was all just background noise to me. I can still hear it all, but the silence is louder. The silence as I stared at my dad and couldn't even comprehend what I was looking at.

I vividly remember being told there was a good chance he may never wake up. I will never forget that fear.

What the fuck just happened in this already fucked-up life?

A severe traumatic brain injury (TBI) consisting of a diffuse axonal injury (DAI), a sub-arachnoid hemorrhage (SAH) and multifocal intraparenchymal hemorrhages (IH). A Glasgow coma scale (GCS) of three. That was the diagnosis. And I studied TBIs in internship as part of my research component—how stupidly ironic—so holy shit, did this feel a bit too familiar.

I could see the charts I had reviewed of TBI patients in my mind from that exact hospital. I could see the words: *paralyzed, never woke up, vegetative state, non-verbal, memory loss, inability to eat or drink, tube fed for life, wheelchair bound, loss of bowel function, can't get off the ventilator, brain dead.* I thought of those patients I had studied, and I could not believe I was looking at one of them right now.

I remember telling my dad about these chart reviews during my research project. He was shocked at the stories. I vividly remember him turning to me and saying, "promise me you won't ever let me live like that."

I won't dad. But at this point, I'm still hoping to God you'll defy the odds.

My mom tapped my arm and asked what these terms meant. Although she was a nurse and knew medical terminology more than the average person, she didn't specialize in neurology. I knew what the terms meant; I knew what the GCS score meant. Fifteen is a perfect score, a healthy brain with eye opening, verbal response, and motor response all working appropriately. Below an eight is comatose, below a three is brain dead. The numbers were bad, really bad. In fact, they were the worst you could score. I remember thinking, *you'll either die or be a vegetable.* The idea of either made me physically ill.

Just like that, the major pillar in my life was removed.

I thought of all the people I wanted to call for extra support, their names dancing through my head. There were coast friends (aka family to me), dietetic friends, UBC friends, soccer friends, family friends… I needed their support, but I could barely fathom building up the mental clarity and capacity to repeat the story that many times. I called only my closest people, between episodes of my emotional state getting the best of me.

We still don't know how it happened, and he will likely never remember it; our brains protect us from remembering that kind of trauma. He was found in the ditch, off his bike, unresponsive. The police ruled out a car hitting him, but we already figured that didn't add up. They ruled out heart attack and stroke when he arrived at VGH. He didn't make a sound so it didn't make sense an animal came out and hit him; I'm sure people from across the water would have heard him swearing his ass off as he fell from his bike, if that was the case. They estimated it was about thirty minutes he was laying there before he was seen. That made my heart ache, but it was shocking his unconscious body somehow kept him alive until help arrived. They took him back up to Shirley Macey, the soccer field, and intubated immediately, meaning at that point he wasn't breathing. I think if the paramedics were there even five minutes later, he would have been dead at the scene. I was beyond grateful for these paramedics, and for the woman who found him and called 911.

His injuries seemed to show he didn't protect himself as he fell, which meant he had likely already lost consciousness or control by the time he fell down. A seizure. It was the only thing that made sense. He had been heading the ball in soccer his whole life, but it's possible that as he aged, his body became less and less able to bounce back from those hits. This repeated trauma likely led to a small bleed in his brain, causing irritation, which caused a seizure.

Why the hell that would happen when he was on the thirty second ride home down the hill on his bike is beyond me; maybe lactic acid in the muscles and the combination of a beer (or two, or three) after the game played a role too. Who knows. It's extremely disturbing not knowing exactly what happened to him.

He stayed the night in emergency. Kat and I figured that as much as Dad was a priority, we needed to remain aware of Mom's state and be strategic in managing her disease, too. She had just come off four months of sober time and was doing well at home, but this was enough to knock anyone off a good track.

We decided it was critical for Mom to get a good sleep. If I was sleep deprived, at least I wasn't at risk of relapsing like she was. But we didn't want her going to Kat's alone because Kat had alcohol at her place. So, the best plan was to split for the night: Kat went with mom to get some sleep at her place, and I stayed with dad.

I slept on his legs. I didn't care about good sleep at that point; I refused to leave him. I was there for the long haul.

Dad got moved up to the Intensive Care Unit (ICU) at four a.m., and I went up with him. I watched every move as they unplugged his ventilator and swapped it for the bag so they could transport him upstairs and use the ventilator in his ICU room. That image of someone holding the bag at his mouth and pushing on it to mechanically give him breaths was just too surreal. It was such a harsh reminder that he physically couldn't breathe on his own, and if someone stopped pushing air into him, he'd die.

Mom and Kat arrived in the morning, and I showed them the ICU room dad was in. Just before the three of us could walk through the sliding glass doors to his room, a nurse put her hand out to stop us. She claimed only two people were allowed in the room. Considering it was a massive room, and the three of us were desperately needing each other's support at this time, I found it absurd that this wasn't an obvious time to make rule exceptions. I argued. She proceeded to repeat herself, this time with a power-trip-non-empathetic tone. Kat says it was at this moment that I started lifting my arm with a tight fist in my hand, a guess the start to a punch in the face? Before I knew it, I was being pulled into a room by my mom and sister to calm down. Shortly after, one of the head Intensive Care Physicians, Dr. Griesdale, came in, a disapproving look on his face in my direction.

"That type of behaviour is unacceptable in this ICU" he said.

My dad's state is unacceptable, I felt like saying, but bit my tongue and nodded in agreement instead.

Dr. Griesdale was a fantastic physician, and this was a good reminder that I needed to stay calm. The team was on our side, and I needed to trust they would do anything they could to save him. It was just really hard to see him so lifeless: big black eye, bloody nose, missing tooth, right cheek fracture, broken shoulder, scratches over his hands, occipital bone fracture, intubated and completely helpless, eyes shut, no response, tubes hooked all over his body, machines breathing for him, and monitors reading every vital measurement you could possibly want. The beeping. So much beeping from the machines. I never thought I would see him like this, and it was traumatic, to say the least.

I didn't sleep, work out, or eat much for a few days. I don't think I'd ever experienced lack of appetite in my life before; it's amazing what stress will do to the body.

The idea that there was a very small chance that he would return to my life was unbearable. We were told it was around a three percent chance. I clung onto that three percent desperately. I remember thinking I just couldn't go on without him. I didn't want a future wedding if he couldn't walk me down the aisle. I didn't want kids in my life if they couldn't have him as a grandpa. I didn't have motivation to accomplish anything more if he couldn't be there cheering me on. I felt I just couldn't do life without him, I refused to.

LIFE IN THE ICU

The teams in ICU were different than any doctors, nurses, or interdisciplinary others that I had ever met. These individuals were world-renowned; people would die to meet them, and they were our doctors. They were the cream of the crop, the best of the best. Unfortunately, that also meant that Dad was one of the most critical patients in the hospital, but he was in the best of hands. Some of our attendings were the guys who invented the bolt that was in drilled into Dad's brain to measure intracranial pressure (ICP) and oxygenation status (O2). These guys were world-class neurologists, neuro, and trauma surgeons. That gave me hope.

We were in rounds every single day. This was where all the team members—attendings, fellows, residents, nurses, pharmacists, dietitians, social workers, physiotherapists (PT), occupational therapists (OT), respiratory therapists (RT), epileptologists—got around Dad's bed and discussed updates and next steps. Things change hourly in the ICU, so every morning and evening they did rounds on all their patients.

It was incredible to watch how organized the team was. The nurse would first give their report of the last eight to twelve hours, which included a detailed head-to-toe report—probably more than Dad ever wanted us to know —including whether or not he was feverish, the temperature of his skin, meds he had been given and his response, any edema and how it was managed, whether there was any movement or response to verbal or physical stimulus, tolerance to the tube feed, how much urine was produced, if bowels were moving or not, his blood pressure, heartbeat, other vitals, and much more.

The other health professionals would give reports if relevant; the dietitian would comment on feeding rate, tolerance, and meeting nutrient needs, the OT would comment on his hand function. The fellow or attending would then challenge his residents on their plan for moving forward—often this included more head CTs or MRIs, a change in meds, another EEG, or referrals to specific specialists to get involved.

I think back to this care, and it still leaves me speechless. It still gives me goosebumps as I feel so lucky and privileged to be in Canada, where we can receive this kind of care when our loved ones are hurt.

It made it so much easier that we were in the healthcare field; Kat was in there with all the meds, and I was all over the tube feed. I asked for a Percutaneous Endoscopic Gastrostomy (PEG) tube to be put in while they were already heading to the OR for the Tracheostomy (trach) insertion. The trach was a longer-term breathing device that carried a lower risk of infection. The PEG was also a longer-term device (for tube feeding) that reduced risk of infection and increased comfort. I knew all this from my prior research project. We were both asking questions in rounds to the doctors about weaning plans and how they planned on managing the current issues. It could be intimidating talking to such top professionals, but we wanted answers to our questions, and we wanted to ensure this recovery was going the way we felt was best for Dad. He couldn't speak for himself, so we had to be his voice.

I also know from working in healthcare that teams are usually aware if patients' families are in the healthcare field, and although there shouldn't be a difference in care, I noticed there was a bit more

71

pep in their step as they came to Dad's room. They were all well aware that Kat and I were very on top of things, and they knew we would have questions daily. I think they even knew I took notes. They assumed we would be following up from yesterday's plans. They came very prepared, and I think this kept them even more on their toes than they already were in this high-intensity job.

We started getting very close to the team, which felt inevitable given we were there every hour of the day. We knew all their names, and they knew ours. They made an extra effort to update us, regardless of how small the update might be. They talked to Dad as if he wasn't in a coma: *okay Dave, now I'm just going to adjust your hip to avoid a bed sore, you're going to feel me lift up... there we go.* I highly respected this, considering I talked to him all the time, still half-expecting a response from his unconscious state.

Kat, mom, and I started writing in a small blue notebook, that I still have today. I'm not sure why but writing felt like a way of coping. I kept track of any daily updates from the team, personal thoughts, or messages to Dad. I've included some examples from the book, one is below:

Thursday, Oct 10ᵗʰ
Day 4

Bolt numbers look good!
- *ICP should be <20 mmHg (yours is ~6-9) – yay!*
- *O2 ideally is >10-15 mmHg (yours is ~18-28) – yay!*
Still sedated to protect the brain from seizures.
X-ray confirmed hand is not broken.
Starting bowel protocol tomorrow.
Eyes look less bruised.
Jerold the pharmacist is a walking Encyclopedia.
Kat apologized to the nurse I almost punched and bought her coffee.

Plan: keep sedated one more day and then try weaning (hopefully no seizures)
Goal: wake the fuck up.

The weaning process was a roller coaster. Basically, when Dad first came in, they were testing how well his brain was able to tell his body how to appropriately respond to pain stimuli. The doctors would have to preform pretty harsh physical stimulus tests to get an accurate idea of how 'awake' his brain was. This included using a pen to push down on his fingernails and toenails, hoping to see him pull his hands and feet away quickly and abruptly. He didn't move much in response to this test, which was very concerning.

They performed sternal rubs—rubbing their knuckles roughly against his sternum—which is supposedly very painful. The normal response to this would be arms and legs immediately and forcefully coming inwards to protect the chest. He didn't respond nearly as well as we hoped, but he did move slightly in response to the stimulus, which provided a small sense of hope. This meant his brain was able to detect some form of extreme pain and try to move away from it.

They had to run these tests a couple times a day, and after witnessing them for the first time, I had to leave the room for the rest. All his fingernails and toenails were black from bruising, and his chest was now an open bleeding wound from the sternal rubs. It was brutal to see them cause him these injuries, but they needed to do it to get an idea of where he was sitting cognitively.

Then he started having seizures, which were only detectable with the EEG wires that were glued to his head. He had to be on maximum doses of five anti-epileptic drugs to control them, which ultimately put him into a comatose state due to the sedative effects of the medications. So, then the weaning game started: weeks of slowly bringing down the meds, by miniscule amounts daily, and hoping he didn't seize.

The problem? He seized. A lot. This meant they had to bump up the meds again to protect his brain. They tried this weaning process a few times. And then there was a point where one of the doctors said, "This isn't looking very good", verbalizing the fear we'd had since day one in the ER that this might not go our way. The issue was that if he couldn't get off the medication without seizing, he would never come out of the coma, which meant he would never come back to us.

Friday, Oct 18th
Day 12

There's no way you go out this early, Dad. You still have to see my graduation. You still have to be there for our futures. You still have a whole life ahead of you to be a grandpa. You still have so many opportunities to tell us we're wrong and you're right. So don't go now. You have to be in our lives. We can't do this without you.

Keep fighting, Dad.

That was the day I told him to smarten up; snap out of this, walk it off, and fight his ass off right now. I told him what the doctor said: that things don't look great and we're trending in the wrong direction. I begged him to give it all his strength one last time while they weaned again the next day. I let him know that this may be his last chance.

Kat went in after me and gave her own version of a pep talk. Begging for some glimmer of hope for this next wean.

I panicked that evening. I got to my car. It was raining. And I fucking lost my mind. I was hyperventilating. I considered walking back to VGH just to admit myself for some fucking oxygen. I've never had a full-on panic attack, but I guess that was it.

It felt horrible. I could hardly breath at the thought of my dad not waking up, and that was a very real and very possible situation we were facing. That may have been the first time I let myself consider that possibility without being in full denial of the severity of the situation. *Fuck, Dad, for the love of god, wake up. You're a fighter. This is NOT how you go out.*

I went to a church that evening and prayed. I literally had no idea what I was doing until I was at the door and the man let me in saying there were no sessions that evening but if I wanted, I could sit in the church. So, I did. I sat in the very front row. No one was around. It was silent. I didn't even know what to do, what to say, where to look. How the fuck do people pray? Is there a proper way?

I just spoke to whoever—God, I suppose—and just said how important my dad is to us, that we physically, mentally, emotionally could not lose him. That he was the glue that kept this messed up family together. That he had been our main parent since Mom's addiction started. That he was the best person I had ever met, and I just prayed and verbalized that I would give anything to save his life. Anything.

The next day they started a fourth weaning—no seizures. They kept going, slowly, over days and weeks, and that was it. No more seizures. I got goosebumps when the nurse told me. I knew he could hear me. *Fuck yeah, Dad. Keep it up.*

Saturday, Oct 19ᵗʰ
Day 13

Weaning Dilantin.
Ideally will be off Clobazam by Nov 5ᵗʰ, will then do another EEG to confirm no seizures.
Chest X-ray looked better but still fighting pneumonia. Still on antibiotics (note: consider probiotics)

The nurse today was a little less chatty, but it's nothing to raise my fist about.

I keep telling you funny stories and I'm not going to lie; I'm getting pretty sick of you not responding... how rude.

Kat is working hard in school, getting great marks, as usual. The only thing pushing her through is knowing you'd want her to keep grinding - you'd be really proud of her.

John Rainer brought by a pigs jersey today for your room.

I miss you every single day.

The hope was that the more we weaned, the more likely he was to wake up, depending on the severity of the injury, of course. So, we waited. We waited, and waited, and waited. We visited every day, and we waited. Some days it was harder than others, like the day they tried to sit him upright and I saw his lifeless body go limp while they transferred him in a sling from the bed to the wheelchair and continued to be limp upon settling in the chair. The whole time his eyes were shut, and his jaw gave way to gravity, hanging open. The most non-Dave look I had ever seen. Some days were a bit easier; having any updates of positive news and talking to him about it. I could watch him for hours, while holding his hand. It was actually amazing how long I could spend staring at his blank face, listening to the sound of the ventilator take breaths for him. Suddenly it was dinner time, and I realized I should probably eat something. It was just really, really hard to leave him.

I guess I'm more similar to my dad than I thought. I have that Nanson grit, or as Kat puts it, "That fierce loyalty to those that you love." And when it comes to my dad, holy shit, watch out world,

I will stand in your way until he is treated in a way that meets my expectations. I understand this attitude has its faults, but it comes in handy when you are advocating your heart out for someone.

Yes, I had an incident where I almost punched a nurse—but hey, I didn't punch her, so that was good. And yes, I told a charge nurse that Dad was not going to be taken care of by a certain nurse again, because she disregarded a potential eye infection (he only has one so maybe that should have been a higher priority.. if he did wake up, you think we need total blindness on top of whatever other deficits he's going to have? Ugh). And yes, I confronted a trauma surgeon on his beliefs about keeping another attending around, who was the best neuro doctor we had ever had, so I advocated to keep him. And yes, there was one more incident where we refused to have a nurse because he forgot (more than once) to buckle dad's wheelchair straps up which felt critical (trying to avoid another head injury here). And yes, when the idea of shipping him to long term care came up, my response was *absolutely not.* I knew in my heart that long term care would be the last stop, in a bad way.

"If you ship him to long term care, it's game over and you know it. If the problem is needing more physio, more occupational therapy, more rehab in general... it doesn't make sense to me to send him somewhere where he'll have *less* of that. I have a mother in rehab, and I can't handle a father in long term care. He stays here."

Silence from the team around the table, and some wide-eyed looks.

Realizing my stern tone, I try again: "can he please stay here until he improves? I'm begging you."

Silence from the team again. Silence and then nods in agreement.

So yes, I got aggressive a few times, but all warranted in my opinion. It wasn't just being entitled and demanding unfair levels of treatment. I'm in healthcare, I know better than to do that to my fellow employees. It was rather a few cases of feeling his care could have shifted the direction of his recovery, that was what scared me.

My dad would have done the same thing if it was Kat, Mom, or me in that bed, unable to advocate for ourselves. And I'd do it all again—I can't help myself when it's his health and life on the line, that's just the way it is. And to be clear, the care was overall amazing, a few bumps in the road was nothing in the grand scheme of things.

Monday, Nov 4th
Day 29

I called your boss today, turns out you have 1.5 years of sick time… I'm starting to believe all the times you told us you hadn't been sick for "20 years."

Julie the nurse was so excited to temporarily take the EEG off today to give you a good head wash.

I caught of glimpse of your calf today, the skin dangling off the back of it as I raised your foot up. All the muscle has just vanished.

We put on some music for you: The Beatles, Neil Young, Bob Marley. I can picture you on the front lawn with a beer in your hand, tapping your foot to the beat until the sun went down.

I miss you so much.

YOU NEED A HAIRCUT SO BAD.

During Dad's recovery, Kat was chipping away at her master's degree. She contemplated for so long whether to continue her schooling, as she had just barely started when he had his accident. I reminded her that if she stopped, and he did in fact wake up, he would kick her ass all the way to Sunday for dropping an important commitment for him. But more importantly, he would simply never forgive himself for what she lost in his recovery. She spent days and weeks beside his hospital bed, studying. I took a month off work to just be there and get my bearings.

I hoped my dad knew this isn't his fault. No one could have predicted his accident. Of course we worried, and it was beyond stressful, but that wasn't his fault. If he wasn't such an incredible human, maybe we wouldn't have cared as much.

After Dad's accident, Kat was onto me about starting counselling again. It had been a while since my UBC counselling experiences, and she wanted me to get a counsellor in the city to see regularly, to start fresh.

I think it was the first time I didn't argue with her about it. My mental state was getting the best of me and the stress I was under was being fired directly at her. I felt angry all the time, and since we were around each other all the time, a lot of that got taken out on her. So, I figured I owed it to her to try. I should have been taking counselling more seriously years ago with Mom, and now that Dad was in a coma, I was broken. I needed it more than ever. So, although I still felt stubborn about it, I just said "okay" without too much of a fight.

I walked away from the first two counsellors I met. I guess I just didn't feel a good vibe from either of them. I remember telling Kat that I was done, I had tried and it didn't work. She pleaded with me to give it one more go, so I begrudgingly went back for a third time and found someone incredible.

Her name is Noa. She had worked with addiction in the past. She agreed not to give me the *Aww*, pat-on-the-back-type counselling, rather, she would interrupt me, tell me if I was wrong, and how I could do better. This was my request because I just felt it was more my style. I do better with the tough love approach.

Right away her jaw dropped when I told her what was going on. She held my pain like it was her own, and she immediately felt like a friend. I decided to start seeing her regularly. There was just something about her I really liked.

And I continued to see her regularly. I finally understood how necessary this was. I don't look at it as a failure anymore, nor a sign of weakness. In fact, I see it now as sign of strength and courage. Asking for help isn't easy, and to acknowledge you need it is coming face to face with the stigmas and saying, "Nah, I don't buy that."

Okay fine Kat, you were right.

THE GIFTS OF COMMUNITY

Everyone from the coast wanted to visit. And I mean everyone. I was beginning to think Dad had more friends than me. Not sure how I felt about that, but that's another story.

These people were beside themselves; everyone just respects him so much. It's like he's a king.

The community on the coast started a committee. They organized a big event at the 101 Bar for him—they sold out of tickets the first day. They signed jerseys, signed cards, and spent time getting together to pray for him. I just couldn't believe the love people had for him. Well, I guess I could. But I don't think many people get this reaction when they get hurt. His friend Bob couldn't stop pacing his house. His friend John cried his eyes out. His friend Ian said this was the worst week of his life, and that he didn't play soccer or drink beer anymore because "There's just no point without Dave." He also said if Dad does wake up to forget the accident, he "surely won't forget scoring his beautiful header goal that game." The devastation among the community was nothing short of amazing.

So naturally, everyone wanted to visit. We had very strict rules about this because we knew Dad would hate people seeing him in such a vulnerable state. We created a visitors list of family only, plus a few others we knew he would be okay with. That's it. Every time someone asked, we had to consider if it was something he would be okay with, and most of the time the answer was no.

His friends and the coast community were unreal. Not only did they do fundraisers, card signing, and jersey making, but they also took care of our house on the coast by cutting the lawn, cleaning the gutters, sweeping the driveway, and shoveling the snow. They put up Christmas lights over the holidays when we couldn't be there because they knew Dad always liked the house to look like someone was home. They were so practical and always thought of the right things to do. They were even brainstorming how they would help renovate the house to make it wheelchair accessible, if in fact Dad did wake up and was unable to use his legs.

They started a challenge in June called "The Soames to Everest Challenge." It was actually the principal at Chatelech High School, Mark Sauer, and his wife, Dana Sauer, who started it. Mark claimed Dad's drive and resolve to get better was what drove him into action.

It was a fitness challenge, aiming to go up Soames—a hill with many stairs in our hometown—seventy-two times in the month of June to equal the distance of climbing Mount Everest. It was a way the community felt they could challenge themselves mentally and physically to support how Dad was being challenged mentally and physically in his daily rehab. Their goal was to raise four thousand dollars. They raised over thirteen thousand. The money went into a bursary in Dad's name for high school students on the coast facing adversity, called the "Soames to Everest Bursary."

People were so motivated to be a part of this journey. I had friends from Vancouver reaching out wanting to donate but do their own fitness challenge in June from town. I had friends from the coast texting me pictures of the signs on the trail to help motivate them and remind them why they were doing this. 'Doin' it for Dave' was one of the signs halfway up.

The first year of this challenge, I was still in Vancouver with Dad, not quite ready to make the move home. But I was excited to be able to participate the following year. What a true honor and privilege to witness his recovery be so inspiring to everyone around him. He is making a huge difference in everyone's lives, and now in the lives of young kids struggling, too. Humbling, to say the least.

We are so lucky to be from such a great town.

LEAVING THE ICU

Dad was in the ICU for about two months. Two months of no conversation, no eye opening, no breathing on his own, no response. It was like tossing a coin to know if he was going to wake up.

One of the nurses came up to me one day and said, "You know, I don't know your dad at all, but seeing how amazing you and your sister are with his care just goes to show how incredible of a dad he must be." I mean, she's not wrong. He is incredible.

Balancing Dad's recovery with Mom's was a lot. Like, a lot. She was trying so, so hard. She was really, really motivated for a while, doing meetings, seeing Dad, and taking care of us. But of course, that just wasn't sustainable.

Yes, there were relapses, and really, really dark times. Things that are difficult to write about. I never thought at age twenty-five I would be taking care of both my parents, calling the cops on one and holding the other one's hand hoping he would wake up. But I would do it over and over again if it meant a chance at a future.

I'm not going to lie, it wasn't easy. I wanted to be at Dad's bedside all the time, but I knew Mom needed help, too. After all, she experienced some trauma here that we didn't: the scene of the accident. Dad's friend, Ian, came to pick him up after the soccer game to go to Blackfish with the guys. When he got to the door, mom told him Dad wasn't home yet. They both seemed puzzled as they realized all Dad had to do was bike down the hill, meanwhile Ian went home to shower and change before coming to pick Dad up. How was Dad not home yet? Mom started walking up the trial to look for him when she heard the sirens. She panicked. She followed them to the scene where Dad was in the ditch. A horrible thing to witness.

Mom was okay, but just needed help coping. I can't imagine going through Dad's recovery on top of the struggle of addiction. I did feel really bad for her, but it was incredibly hard to go through these relapses without him, it made me realize how much he did. Kat and I could do it—we knew how—but we also just wanted to have our mom be more or less normal as we went through this tragic time with Dad. It was rough, to say the least.

Mom couldn't be there during Dad's recovery because she needed to be in treatment. She tried coming to visit when she was slipping, and I knew it was a recipe for disaster. She wasn't mentally well enough to see him in that state; it was causing her to spiral.

I didn't feel comfortable having her in the room when she wasn't in her right mind. I knew how erratic she could act when she was using. I was worried she would accidentally unplug a tube or lie on his IV line. I hated having to take a stand and enforce a barrier, but it was for everyone's safety. Eventually, I had to make the difficult decision to put Mom on the 'do not visit' list. It was painfully hard to forgive myself for doing that, but I know I had to, at least for the time being.

The irony of this was knowing how good she would be in this role without her addiction. Not only was she well equipped with her nursing background, but she had a natural ability to go the extra mile for someone in need. She would have been right there in the hospital with Kat and I every single day. She would have advocated with us during rounds. She would have ensured we had food and coffee (for Kat) to keep us going. She would have been the leader of the group. I was sad thinking of how different this would be if she wasn't suffering with addiction. This damn disease took her away from us during this time and forced us to put up boundaries we hated ourselves for.

Finally, Dad started to turn a corner. The status had been the same day in and day out, without a glimmer of significant improvement. Then suddenly, his lungs were starting to slowly wake up, starting to breathe on their own a little bit. This meant there was no need for the ventilator. Removal of the ventilator was a huge step in recovery because if a patient can't breathe on their own, they are bound to this breathing machine forever, and most families choose to pull the plug at that point. Getting rid of the ventilator meant moving from the ICU to the Burns Trauma High Acuity (BTHA) Unit. Although he had remained in the coma at this point, he was one step closer to potentially coming back to us. This move was a step in the right direction, and we were willing to take any of those we could get.

Good news started to come, as he opened his eyes a few weeks later. What was strange was that he wasn't registering what was in the room. This was a bizarre thing to see. He was looking straight forward: no emotion, no movement, no life. I remember snapping my fingers inches from his face: no reaction. I remember moving my hand from left to right in front of his eyes: no tracking. It was indescribably weird to see him in this state, it's like he was in a trance.

That blank stare haunts me. The team explained this was part of the normal process of waking back up; it is one of the steps in brain injury recovery, making it "normal." It felt like the furthest possible thing from normal. We still weren't sure how much he would recover, but whatever recovery we do see will come in stages like this. It will be slow, that we know for sure.

The biggest issues now were requiring Optiflow—warmed air—and having multiple secretions throughout the day which required lots of suctioning. This basically meant he couldn't quite control his own secretions, so they had to suction him every hour.

What the hell is suctioning? Glad you asked. It's when they push a tube in the trachea site down into your lungs until it forces a cough reflex and the gunk from your lungs comes up through the tube when you cough. It was weird seeing him cough forcefully when he wasn't really awake yet. It was like he was coughing but not from his mouth, rather from the trach site in his throat. It was a very strange thing to see.

The more I saw, the more I was baffled by how much our body does for us on a daily basis. Without thinking, our hearts beat, pushing blood around our body to oxygenate our tissues. Our lungs breathe in fresh oxygen and discard used carbon dioxide. Our liver metabolizes while our kidneys excrete waste. Our brains are working to control every physical movement and every mental thought. And we simply take this for granted every day. Have you ever woken up in the morning and just thought, *thank you heart, thank you for beating and keeping me alive...* probably not. Maybe you should start.

Eventually, Dad started to move his eyes a little bit. I will never forget one day when he looked right at me—but was it at me, or right through me? It was hard to tell with that vacant stare thing still going on.

I will also never forget the day he moved his left arm. He hadn't moved his arms at all yet, the most we had gotten was a twitch in his left calf. It was the day before my graduation, and it was the biggest heartache going without my dad. I told him again about the accident, I told him not to be scared, I told him I didn't even want to go to graduation without him, and I told him that I missed him so, so much. And at that moment of verbalizing that I missed him, while he continued to stare blankly forward, he brought his hand up to my shoulder. I started bawling. I knew he heard me, and I knew he was responding, in the only way he could. This arm movement was his way of telling me to go graduate, to go celebrate, and that he was proud. I can't even describe that feeling, it was so fucking surreal.

I had only two tickets. I had to choose wisely, but it was pretty clear it would be Mom and Kat who got seats to my graduation ceremony. I wasn't pleased with Mom's behavior, but how could I not invite her to my graduation? She was struggling, she couldn't bear to go to any big life event without my dad by her side, so she drank. She drank to forget. She drank to ease the pain and suffering. She drank the morning of grad and didn't make it.

I worked hard for my degree for seven years. My dad was one of the most important people who could have been there, so it was sickening enough that he wasn't. I barely wanted to go knowing he wouldn't be watching me cross that stage, something he had waited for... for so damn long. He was so excited that he had asked me the date of it repeatedly earlier that year. But to have my other, physically available parent, not show up for me was devastating. I guess she wasn't mentally available.

I will never forget looking up at those empty seats from the stage. My sister was the only family I had there and thank god for her. Looking up to see her smiling face and clapping hands was the only thing that got me through that day. She carried me through what I couldn't carry myself through. But I had been let down again. And this time, it was a big loss. This was a big life event for me, one that I'll never experience again. What would she miss next, my future wedding? My first born child? Their graduation?

Like I said, addiction is powerful. My mother would never have let me down in her right mind. She would never have had me in tears on that day. She would never have chosen alcohol over my graduation. But the addict would. And the addict did.

MYPSTER

Dad's entire medical team was amazing, but one doctor in particular went above and beyond. His name was Mypinder, or Myp for short. Or Mypster, as written on his white lab coat.

He came by the ICU and had Dad as his patient for only four days. I remember the first time I saw him; he was in biking gear as he had ridden his bike to work that day. I remember him peeking in the room, and I thought, *who the hell is this guy? Doesn't look like one of the medical team members.*

Sure enough, he was. In fact, he was an intensive care physician and neuro-intensivist. Personally, I found it easier to consider him a neurologist, even though that wasn't an entirely accurate title. He noticed that Kat and I were alone, and how upset we were. He saw this image of two young girls with the biggest pillar in their life removed and lying in a bed with machines breathing for him. He decided from that moment on that he was going to take the lead in Dad's care—he was going to be there for us as someone stable to depend on.

He showed us all Dad's MRI and CT scans and explained what was actually happening in the brain. *See all these little white dots? That's blood. See how the blood is sitting all over his brain, but especially on this area here, which is critical for consciousness, so it makes sense he's not awake.* He made it make so much sense. And there was something about his demeanor that gave me hope for Dad's recovery.

Kat's boss wasn't understanding of why she needed time off work, what an asshole... probably a good thing I never ran into her. I vividly remember Myp's response. We explained what Kat's boss had said, which was "You're not sick, your dad's sick, so why can't you come into work."

Silence. I remember thinking, *Ah shit, we told him too much. Maybe he knows her, or maybe he thinks we're being dramatic. Damn, shouldn't have said it.* And then I laughed so hard when Myp's response was, "Fuck that. What's her contact? I'll send her a letter." I thought, *yup we're going to get along just fine.*

So, he wrote Kat's boss a letter explaining how head injuries work and how Kat needed time off to be there for her dad as part of a successful recovery for him, as well as mental health for her.

Myp asked if there was anything he or the team could do for Mom. There never was anything anyone could do for her, but just to have him ask felt incredible.

He reviewed Dad's chart and test results over and over to try to find more answers. And he promised he would continue to follow us after these short four days of having Dad as his patient, which, to be honest, I thought was total BS. What kind of doctor continues to follow someone that isn't their patient and that most trauma doctors likely don't have time for?

Turns out he wasn't kidding. He showed up at least weekly to ensure whichever doctor was overseeing Dad's care was working to our expectations. He checked in on Kat and I and reassured us about Dad's state and progress. He helped us feel better when we were worried. He assured us Dad's goal was GF Strong, even if it didn't feel like he was close to that point yet. GF Strong was one of the best-known rehabilitation facilities in the country, focusing primarily on brain and spinal injuries. This place was his best shot of a good recovery, if he could eventually get accepted.

In fact, one day a social worker reminded me how difficult it was to get into GF Strong, and not to worry because, "There are decent rehab centers in Alberta, too." ALBERTA?! OHHH OKAY YEAH LET ME JUST QUIT MY JOB, PACK MY SHIT, HOP ON A PLANE, AND HEAD TO ALBERTA! OH, AND IF I CAN'T GO, MAYBE I CAN SEND MY ALCOHOLIC MOTHER WITH HIM. BEST OF LUCK, GUYS!

You have got to be kidding me. So naturally, I went to Myp and told him how scared I was about this potential 'casually move to another province' idea. Myp said if that ever happened again, I was to call him. He reassured me that Dad's goal was GF Strong, and he would make it there. Myp was in our corner, and he really, really cared. He was still seeing Dad as a patient even though he wasn't his patient anymore. I was blown away by his commitment to us, and to Dad. He saw how much Dad meant to us, and he was as determined as us to bring him back.

WHISPERS OF HOPE

Dad was in the BTHA area for about one month, and then things turned around again, and he was able to be moved up to the ward. This was huge. Going up to the ward meant he didn't need any breathing assistance anymore, and he didn't need the extra resources that they only had in the ICU/high acuity units. This was really great news. This was another step in the right direction.

He had started to track with his eyes a bit, which was another positive step. But he still wasn't talking. The same trauma doctors followed him up to the ward, but we had a whole new team of nurses, PTs, OTs, Care Aids, Dietitians, Social Workers, and Care Coordinators.

We got really close with the PT, Aly, and the OT, Emily—they were incredible, and they loved Dad. I swear they spent more time with him than any other patient. They saw our commitment to him, and they tried to match it. I tell ya, being here twenty-four/seven did pay off. They worked with him every day for movement and trying to build back strength, even in those early stages of barely waking.

Uncle Mike and Auntie Patti still came every Saturday. Dad usually sat in a wheelchair in the day, as he wasn't yet able to hold his body up in a seated position on his own. Sometimes his back would start to hurt so he would have to go back to bed. One day, he was really uncomfortable, and I wondered if it was his back. So, I got real close to his face, looked him right in the eyes, and asked, "Dad, is it your back?" and he whispered, through gritted teeth, "Yes."

This was his first time saying a word, even though it was a whisper. It was so exciting. I said, "DID YOU HEAR THAT!?" to Uncle Mike, who was sitting beside us. I was so *fucking excited*. It was another step in the right direction.

I never thought I'd be in a place in my life where a whisper from my dad's mouth made me jump for joy, but there we were.

Whispers. All whispers now. This was all his voice would allow him to do at this time. It was very hard to hear him, and we had to lean in quite close. We didn't always make out what he was saying because it was all a mumbled sentence, but we tried so hard to understand him. Sometimes we said, "Pardon?" three times, and then he just said, "Fuck." It wasn't funny per se, but it was nice to see his personality come back.

"Fuck" became one of his favorite words. He had days where he swore, a lot. I could often see his gritted teeth behind anything he was trying to say. I can't imagine how frustrating it was going from an athlete and independent man to learning how to speak again— not being able to think of the words you want to say, and not being able to use your voice when you want to, and not understanding why. I empathized with this. And this is the normal progression of a brain injury; you go through phases, and one of them is agitation.

One day he leaned forward, so Kat and I leaned forward too—as we did to get ready to try to make out what he was going to say— and he whispered, "Get me the fuck out of here." This was hilarious. Such as classic thing for him to say. I think some part of his brain was realizing he was in the hospital, in a wheelchair, in a hospital gown, and thought, *nope, I don't like this, so get me the fuck out of here.* Part of me felt sad that he was probably confused as to why he was there, but I had to focus on the good: this was his personality shining through.

It must have all felt like a bad dream to him.

I was still a little worried about him remembering us, it really freaked me out. I got caught in the little wins that we had, like limb movement, eye tracking, and then whispering. But then I remembered that I still wasn't sure he knew who we were.

I looked him right in the eye one day and said, "Dad, you know who I am, right?"

He just stared at me in silence. Not even a nod. What's the point if we have to start over? How do you live a life in which this person you love so much doesn't know you anymore? What a *fucking nightmare* of a thought. I think I threw up shortly after that moment.

But then he did start to say our names, and that was an undeniably memorable moment.

Me: "Dad, who am I?"

Dad: "Beth."

Long pause.

Dad: "Bethy."

Okay I think I just died and went to heaven. Wow. Holy shit. Thank god. From that point on it was clear he knew who we were. I was so relieved. I walked down the road to the bakery with the biggest smile on my face and bought myself a goddamn dark chocolate chip cookie.

I remember Mike came the next day, still uncertain if Dad would remember him—long story for another time but we have quite a history of family drama and we didn't see our dad's siblings for a long, long time—so we sat down and I said, "Dad, who's this?" pointing to Uncle Mike. And he goes, "It's Mike," while raising his hand as if it was the stupidest question I could have ever asked him.

I could see how happy that made Mike. You just never think you'll be in a position where your brother saying your name is such a goddamn relief.

Tuesday, Dec 10th
Day 65

Today was the best day ever. You knew who we were.

I asked to change your tube feed to the higher fiber option, and they agreed (Dietitian things...)

I finally showered!

Note: ask neuro if Keppra is giving him nightmares.

Note: get more omega 3's to add to the tube feed. The high DHA one for brain health.

GOODBYE, 2019

Christmas would never be the same without Dad; what a weird experience. He had always loved Christmas, which made it easier to simply write off this year because there was absolutely no point in celebrating it without him. I had never hated Christmas before. Christmas 2019 was the worst.

I gained empathy for people that don't like the holidays because it reminds them of the grief they had in the past. I finally got that. I felt sick thinking of all the people that just try to get through the holidays rather than being able to enjoy them. Until then, I had never thought about people not liking this wonderful time of year.

Kat and I both put on a pair of hospital socks to match his and watched a Christmas movie with him, each on one side of his wheelchair, and I remember just hoping for a better holiday next year.

It's interesting thinking about the meaning of holidays, and how that changes when you experience something that alters the way they are perceived. Christmas is a great example of this. What a lovely time full of bright lights, presents, family, good music, warm drinks, fireplace reading, movies until midnight, and satisfying food. This isn't the case for everyone.

For some this is accurate, and for others, it's a time of grief and loss. It's something they want to get through rather than look forward to. This Christmas Dad was severely brain injured and Mom was somewhere using. I didn't care to celebrate. There was nothing to celebrate. I didn't want lights up or a tree because why would we do that without the whole crew there. I didn't want to check social media and see other peoples' fun Christmases. I wanted it over with so, so badly. Another reminder of how privileged I was for so long to not know that feeling before. I had flashbacks of our old Christmas shenanigans: before we stopped believing, dad would be on the roof with his hockey stick, convincing us Santa really was real, and mom would be helping us prepare cookies, milk, and carrots for the reindeer. Even when Kat and I were older, my parents both still loved celebrating Christmas. Mom would spend the whole year collecting stocking stuffers, she started in January, and would find the most incredible things. Dad wouldn't allow Christmas music until December, but once we hit December first, they were on repeat daily. My thoughts continued to trail until the beeping of Dad's dinner tube feed completion snapped me back into the present moment.

Oh, but on a positive note, Myp came by on Christmas Eve AND Christmas Day to check on Dad. Yes, I'll repeat, to check on DAD. And no, he wasn't even working those days.

Another positive note was that dad had passed his swallow assessment. It had been determined it was safe to move onto liquids and a pureed diet, and slowly build to a normal diet ensuring there's no risk of choking. I was hopeful he could make it all the way to normal food.

Along came New Years. Holy shit, see ya fuckin' later, 2019. I had never been so happy to say goodbye to a year before in my life. Too much shit, too much drama, too much addiction and alcohol, too much negativity, and of course, too much trauma and grief.

I was excited for 2020 because I had a feeling it was going to be a good year; I mean, it sort of had to be after all that bullshit, right? Didn't we deserve that? I hoped so. I had big plans for 2020, mostly just involving Dad being back in our lives and being with him as much as we could, celebrating his survival.

From this point on, he started talking more and more. I think I was finally understanding what it must be like to have kids and watch them achieve things like their first steps or their first words. The more he said, the more excited I got, and I have to say I never thought him saying "Hi" would make my heart skip a god damn beat. It was like being a kid on Christmas morning, I just couldn't believe it. He was slowly starting to say more and more, and it was a great feeling because prior to this, we didn't know if he'd ever be able to talk again.

RANCHOS LOS AMIGOS

At the onset of 2020, Myp was still trying to get Dad into GF Strong, but he unfortunately hadn't passed a couple of the assessments. The woman who had assessed him had somehow come and gone without seeing us. There were no notes left so it was difficult to know what we needed to work on to help him improve for the next assessment; we just assumed Dad's inability to follow commands was a big barrier.

I was able to track down her phone number and I left a voicemail asking to be present for the next assessment. I mean, how did she even miss us? We were there twelve hours a day, so she either came overnight (unlikely because... who does that), when we went pee (but I was pretty quick, and Kat and I never went pee at the same time), or when we went to grab lunch (the most likely case... I guess she skips lunch). Strike one for her.

In the next few days, Dad's speed of recovery continued to get better and better. He was now sometimes able to let them know when he had to go to the bathroom, he was talking more, and he was starting to get more mobile.

One of the doctors from the ICU came up because he didn't believe Dad was talking, let alone alive, so he came to see for himself. He came into Dad's room and said, "Hi, Dave." Dad was sitting in the wheelchair, looked over and waved to him and said, "Hi, how's it going?" Although his voice still sounded somewhat robotic and his speech was slowed, the look of total shock on the doctor's face was priceless.

"Incredible," he managed to get out while his face was still frozen in shock. He continued to say: "I didn't want to tell you guys in the ICU because we never really know for sure, but I truly didn't think your dad was surviving this." I thought to myself, *well I'm sure glad you didn't tell me that in the ICU because I wouldn't have held back from my punch-to-the-face that time.*

He said, "Why the heck is this guy still here, let's get him to GF Strong, he's ready." So, he made the call that day for them to come back and complete another assessment.

Recovery from a brain injury is painfully slow. Studies have been done on the cognitive and behavioral patterns brain injured patients go through as they recover from the injury, it's called the Ranchos Los Amigos Scale (RLAS) [1].

The scale is divided into eight categories:

1.   **No response.** This is pretty much as it sounds, no response to stimulus and they usually have a machine breathing for them.
     This was Dad's status for the first three months. Comatose. Lifeless.

2.   **Generalized response**. They are asleep most of the time, but may wake up slightly to noises, movement, or touch.
     I would say this was when Dad was still in the high acuity unit downstairs. He still wasn't really awake but there was some small limb movement happening. I knew somewhere in his brain he could hear our voices, or at least I chose to believe that. I talked out loud to him lots. I reminded him everything would be okay. I could actually see his heart rate come down on the monitor when I told him not to worry, that we were right there with him.

100

3. **Localized response.** Movement of limbs and the body are more frequent. They may be able to respond to stimuli and commands better, but this is still inconsistent.

   I remember Dad being able to move his limbs better, and more on command rather than random twitches. However, there were still days he just wasn't responding, even when he was looking at us in the eyes and seeming to understand what we said. Maybe his brain just couldn't relay the message to his body yet.

4. **Confused—agitated.** Here they have poor memory and are confused most of the day. If speaking, mixing up words is common as well. They are frustrated and show it. The brain is starting to wake up but has difficulty controlling the response to the environment.

   This was a tough phase. He was angry, go figure. Not only do you wake up confused as hell, but even when you are trying to function as a human again you start to realize how much you have lost. He was starting from square one; re-learning shapes and colors, how to dress himself, how to use the toilet, how to walk again, and when those are mastered, it will be re-learning things like how to use a credit card, reset his PINs, how to get gas in a car, how to drive a vehicle, how to get groceries, how to cook, and so on. So, he was angry, wouldn't you be if all your abilities vanished? Imagine every skill you had ever learned just being wiped from your brain. It's a toddler in a fifty-seven-year-old man's body. So, these outbursts—they were hard to see, of course, especially when they were taken out on us, but we had to remember this was part of the recovery process. For this injury, this is normal. This isn't him right now. And pray to god it will pass, and he will move on to the next step of the scale. We just need to better navigate this new normal.

   In was in this phase that we also became aware of his inability to cover up tearful moments. He's shed a tear in front of us once in his lifetime, but now he starts to cry often. If we discuss how lucky he was to live, or how amazing the nursing staff has been, or how much his siblings love him, he starts to well up. Anything sentimental, and he's done for. He doesn't like his change much, but he says he really has no ability anymore to control it.

On days you are convinced the nightmares you're having are real, I will come lay beside you, hold your hand, and remind you they're not.

And on days you piss me off... you'll still see me the next morning. Even if I sit in the corner with my arms crossed. I will still be there because I committed to this journey and I'm not a damn quitter.

5. **Confused—inappropriate—non-agitated.** They are more awake, and follow simple commands better, but are still confused. They have good long-term memory but are very foggy with events since the accident. They are not able to learn new information. They have difficulty with simple tasks such as dressing themselves and eating. And they tend to typically show inappropriate behavior such as sexual comments or actions.

I remember Dad's long-term memory was impressive, but his short-term memory was very poor. It was most notable when we were training him for the GF Strong assessment. They will ask some basic questions like your name, birthdate, where you are, and why you are here. Kat and I would ask Dad these questions, his name was the only one he knew. And when we would remind him of his birthday, tell him he's at the hospital because he hit his head very hard, he would nod, but he wouldn't remember it for when we asked again five minutes later, and would instead give us a blank stare again.

6. **Confused—appropriate.** They are better with simple
    tasks here, and their attention is much improved; typically
    able to hold attention for as long as thirty minutes. They
    are now appropriate with responses, but the responses are
    very robotic —repetitive with the same answers. They may
    come off as being selfish and are still easily confused.
    The robotic responses stick out in my head. I do remember think-
    ing things sounded very monotone and repetitive. It was beyond
    difficult to hear him sound so different from his normal self.

7. **Automatic—appropriate.** They are now able to do their
    routines without much confusion, but still struggle with
    making good decisions or problem solving anything. They
    have poor insight into these issues. They can now learn
    new information, but at a rate much slower than prior to
    the injury.
    This was more notable when we arrived at GF Strong. He was
    able to get into his scheduled routine easily but was delayed in
    his ability to grasp new concepts from his classes. This did come
    easier with more repetition and time.

8. **Purposeful—appropriate.** Memory is much better here,
    but still impaired with recent events. Their behavior is
    appropriate and good enough to function in social settings.
    Additional problems with thinking and behavior may only
    be noticeable to close friends and family at this point.
    This was exactly the case by the time we were ending our stay
    at GF Strong. He ended up being very functional in social set-
    tings, but as mentioned, the remaining deficits were still notice-
    able to us.

The goal was to get through all eight steps, but the scary thing was
that a patient's recovery could stop at any category, leaving them in
that state more or less permanently.

It would be slow. It was like his brain had a massive bruise in it, and anyone knows how long bruises take to heal, think of your last charley horse. Your brain, however, is so tightly packed and so full of neurons, it takes a lot longer to heal this bruise, if it ever can. It's like a traffic jam: cars bumper to bumper, no-one is moving, there's clear inability to get from point A to point B. The traffic jam in his brain is wired by neurons: they are unable to move properly and can't send the message from Point A to Point B due to the roadblocks of trauma and bleeding. Eventually, like any traffic jam or roadblock, there's detours. The hope in the brain is that it can eventually create its own detours, getting from Point A to Point B via a different route. This is why healing takes so much time, not only is the brain trying to wake up again, but it's trying to form new pathways where the old ones are no longer effective.

At one point, the trauma surgeon and intensivist said to me, "Your dad has made such a good recovery, and the entire team admires your family for how much you've supported him. In a case as severe as his, and with the minimal chance at survival he had, we know for certain you guys are the reason he woke up."

That felt good to hear. It felt incredible to have a world-class trauma surgeon say this. I was speechless. It had been exhausting, so I was beyond thrilled that the lack of sleep and stress beyond any other had paid off. It seemed our voices, touch, and presence by his bedside helped him come back to us. There really is something to be said about the subconscious mind.

Saying goodbye to VGH was bittersweet; sweet because we were moving on to bigger and better things, but bitter because we met a lot of incredible healthcare professionals there, ones we've gotten to know quite well who helped get Dad to where he is today. We said our goodbyes, hugging most of the team members and leaving a basket of goodies and a card to praise their hard work. Many of the top dog doctors were hard to track down upon discharge, managing other critical patients in the ICU, but we knew we'd be back for Dad to meet the ones he hadn't yet. We were on route to the next recovery stop. GF Strong meant he would be meeting a whole new team and stepping foot into a whole new facility. Unknown territory. I knew they would get to know us pretty quick.

GF STRONG

Hello GF Strong (GFS), and what a welcome transition it was. We went with Dad for the transfer because we knew he would be scared on his own: getting wheeled by a random person into a random van taken to a new place and rolled into a new room with bare walls. I don't think so.

We helped set up his new room. As soon as we got there, people were coming in one after another and introducing themselves. Everyone wanted to meet him. We met his team right away.

A full schedule was in the making—mostly OT and PT appointments, but there were balance classes, music classes, and hand classes too. That seemed like a good thing because his right hand was still quite weak. However, he had adapted quite well to using his left hand for teeth brushing and eating. I wondered if maybe he should just be left-handed now.

Dad seemed to really like his OT, Brittany, and PT, Heather; they were incredible with him. They had long appointments with him and gave him their full attention.

Brittany came into his room in the morning and helped him brush his teeth, get dressed, and get into his wheelchair right away. She then took him to the gym where they worked on hand movements and cognitive skills.

I knew these things must have felt so basic to him—like telling time, spelling a word, saying the days of the week—but this was all part of the recovery from a brain injury. I knew he was aware that he was unable to do all these tasks, and it was frustrating because it felt like they should be simple. He probably knew he would normally be able to do them quite easily, so he had to have immense patience to be able to be gentle with himself and understand that it would get better with time. I kept reminding myself that he was through the worst of it. It was time for determination and hard work, two things he was not unfamiliar with in the slightest.

Starting from square one was tricky. Yet another reminder of how much we take for granted every single day when it comes to our health. But they say our brain *may* have a way of adapting and reorganizing its function after this type of injury, that it *could* re-learn tasks and re-route itself to work again. They call this neuroplasticity. This gave me hope.

Dad's personality shone through more every day, and it always put the biggest smile on my face. I sometimes felt that I no longer needed counselling for my messed-up life, all I needed was to see him smiling and hear him laughing and joking with us.

That was a joke - obviously I still do need actual counselling. A lot of it!!

I had been giving him a hard time about not getting out of bed until he pressed the call bell to notify the nurse to assist him. But being a determined and stubborn person, he tried to get up himself. This scared the crap out of me because if he did attempt to get up on his own and fell, which was likely, he could hit his head, and back he would go to the ICU at VGH and may not make it back to GF Strong that time. No thank you.

So, I pointed my finger at him and told him not to get up until the nurse came. He laughed and pointed his finger back while imitating me: "Don't get out of bed Daaaddd." Even though I was serious about my point, seeing him imitate me was hilarious. And again, that's *him*. That's the dad I knew. I loved it.

He agreed to start using the call bell after I explained how it worked. He found it quite fascinating that one press of a button led to a nurse at his bedside within minutes, sometimes even seconds. I had to quickly re-explain when to *appropriately* use the bell after a nurse came running in, to which dad responded "boy, that's wild hey" while looking at me, his thumb still pressed to the red button.

He then saw me biting my nails and told me it was a bad habit that I should quit. We both laughed out loud as he knew he had a terrible nail-biting habit his whole life, which only just subsided post-brain injury. After nothing else had worked to quit, he suddenly woke up from this injury with zero desire to continue chewing his nails.

He was just so funny to be around. One day at lunch, Uncle Mike made some joke that I didn't get because it was of a different era.

"Well Dad, you must get it then" I said.

"Oh yeah, I got it" he replied. "It just wasn't funny."

I could see Mike grinning behind his sandwich.

Earlier that morning, when the social worker came to the room asking what Dad did for work, Dad sarcastically replied "well… not a whole lot right now!" to which we all had a good laugh.

The following week I asked him when his birthday was, and he immediately replied "February third." When I responded with "wow Dad, you remembered it!", he looked to me, confused, and said "well.. YA.. it's my birthday." I just smiled and neglected to tell him he didn't know it four weeks ago.

He had come so far. I knew there were still huge frustrations ahead for him; when he couldn't think of the word he wanted, when he struggled trying to finish a sentence even though he knew what he wanted to say. Telling time was more difficult than it had ever been, he would sit gritting his teeth while staring at the clock, trying to figure out what it meant. Mobility was tricky and his legs reminded him of that every day. He still couldn't use his dominant hand, he couldn't even close it properly around a pen or pencil.

I kept telling him I couldn't imagine what it would be like to go from being an athlete, solid parent, social butterfly, and productive personality, to learning shapes and words again. I knew it must be incredibly frustrating, feeling like he was back in elementary school.

But he also didn't see himself when he was in the coma. He didn't sit by his own bedside day in and day out holding the hand of a loved one hoping they would wake up. He didn't feel beat to exhaustion going to rounds daily and collaborating with the team, advocating his heart out.

I knew his recovery was really, really brutal for him. But for Kat and me, these were minor deficits compared to what we were potentially facing a few months ago. He was awake. He knew who we were. Although we always wanted more recovery, we were beyond grateful for these two things.

Nothing would change the way I looked at him. My dad, the strongest human I know, my role model, my hero. Even more so now that he's survived this un-survivable injury. He will remind me every day how precious life is, how fragile it can be, and how grateful to be.

But I'm really not kidding when I say he's my hero—he's the one I boast about when talking to my friends. All of them know him even if they've never met him because I talk about him, because they are in awe of what he's dealt with in his life, because they know a lot of the strength Kat and I have is from him, and because the ones that have met him see all these wonderful traits for themselves. It just takes meeting him once to admire him in a big way.

It felt like I got a text every day from someone who wanted to come visit Dad. *How were they even getting my number?* It was amazing and humbling what people would do to reach out. It was always difficult to make decisions about who could see him, and we were so careful in the ICU because he could not make his own decisions. However, now that he was able to consent to things, we left it up to him to decide who he was up for seeing and when.

I tried to arrange visits for him between appointments or on weekends when he didn't have programming. Sometimes I just wanted to throw my phone out as it was an added stress to constantly be getting back to people, and it became exhausting. Dad's good friend John Rainer took on the job of relaying messages. He would get updates from us, and then pass them along to large lists of contacts on the coast. This was so helpful because I wanted people to be updated but I barely had energy to get back to more than one person. John referred to me as Dad's security guard; people had to get by me first if they wanted to get to him. I was content with that.

Our time at GF Strong wasn't always pretty; there were massive frustrations during his rehab, which sometimes got taken out on us. I've said it before, and I'll say it one hundred more times: I can't imagine how difficult this injury was for him, and sometimes we saw the consequences of that. It's always like that, isn't it? When we have bad days or go through difficult times, we tend to take some of that out on the ones closest to us.

We are family, we will argue. Not arguing isn't a real relationship between two close people but talking about it and recognizing how both people can do better, is.

I saw him working hard. I saw him pushing and grinding. I would be there to listen to all his frustrations. And no matter how mad I might have been one day, no matter how many times I might have said I wasn't coming back, he would see me the next morning because I would *always* come back. I didn't care if I sat in the corner and didn't talk to him for a few hours because I was mad. I would still be there. I would continue to support him no matter what. No matter how mad I got, I knew we would always work it out. I promised him that.

We had a particularly bad argument when I was at GF Strong one day. I was calling the bank to try and get more information on how to go about re-setting someone's passwords and pins after they've been comatose for three months. I had my cell on speakerphone so that I could multitask with something else, of course. I guess the robotic voice coming from the phone bothered his brain and he just started yelling at me to hang-up. Understandably, I felt defensive as I was only doing things to make his life easier post-discharge. After this argument, we talked for a long time. When I left that night, I said to him, "Dad, you know why we argue sometimes? Because we are the same person."

"Yeah, I know. Goodnight, Dave." Dammit, he cracks me up.

Walking out the doors was never easy. I could spend the entire day with him, going to classes, talking to staff, eating lunch and dinner there so he could avoid playing along with uninteresting conversation in the dining hall—he was so stubborn! I could spend thirteen hours in the facility and still feel the guilt walking out those doors at eight p.m.

I knew I had to leave. We both needed sleep so leaving was the logical thing to do, but it was surprisingly challenging. I felt saddened that he was there alone—only for the next ten hours, of course, until we arrived again in the morning—but the feeling sat heavy with me all night, every night. I didn't want him to be alone, scared, sad, or worried. I didn't want him to wake up from nightmares or forget momentarily where he was and why he was there. I had days that were full of laughs and hope, only to walk out the door with a heavy heart.

I vividly remember walking out of the side doors to the sidewalk and turning to see his room window; sometimes he wasn't there, and I would just look at the jerseys and pictures we put up on his wall from a distance. Sometimes he was sitting there, and we'd wave goodbye. I always had to put a huge smile on my face and wave quickly, because I could feel the tears start as I turned to walk toward the bus stop.

I didn't want him to see me sad, I knew that would break him. I just hated leaving—it felt so wrong that at a young age I was witnessing my dad in a facility with his own room and set of dresser drawers, his own bathroom, his little hospital bed, and his wheelchair parked right beside it. His home away from home.

I had flashbacks of seeing him dribble past me with the soccer ball mumbling, "still too fast for ya, hey, grasshopper?", a sassy smirk on his face. I was quickly shaken back into reality seeing him in this rehab room. I got stuck in the past; I would pinch myself, hoping it was a bad dream, but I knew it wasn't.

His recovery began to move quickly, and I was blown away by the pace.

He had to re-learn how to walk, starting with help from a machine, then walking between bars. I watched the physio as she physically grabbed one leg to help him take a step, planted that foot on the ground, and then grabbed the other leg to help it move forward to complete the step. It was hard to see such a smart, capable, independent man move like a robot, as if his legs were brand new and hadn't had a chance to function yet. It was like he wanted his leg to move forward but his brain said, "Nah, not yet."

He then moved onto walking with a walker or harness around his waist held by the physio. Then, he started walking with a band around his waist held by the physio. Finally, he walked mostly unsupported, holding the physio's hand. Each of these progressions took weeks to accomplish.

He started doing stairs, hands on the rails and a harness around his waist. He could only do about four before his body was shaking with exhaustion, but this was the normal progression for his injury. He laid in a hospital bed for three-and-a-half months, of course his body is going to be weak as hell.

He said he felt the strength slowly but surely coming back in his legs. He still had quite a bit of muscle to regain, but he was on his way. He'd lost about fifty pounds through his VGH stay. Being bedridden long term put his body into a highly catabolic state—breaking down rapidly to try and use energy for healing.

He was starting to write with his dominant hand. It was extremely shaky and scribbly, and you could see the anger on his face while staring at what looked like a four-year-old's printing.

"It will get better, you're doing great" I told him, over and over.

The speech language pathologist not only helped him with pronunciation, but also on word recall, memory, and labelling:

"Okay Dave, what's this?" – she held up a razor.

"A banana" he replied, confidently.

"And what do we do with bananas?" she asked, playing along.

"Put them in smoothies", he smirked at me, clearly remembering how many smoothies he made us at home.

"Great. Thank you" she said. "Let's try another. Let's try to name as many animals as you can within one minute. Go."

"Umm.. chicken, fish, manta ray, chicken again."

We all chuckled a bit here as she told him "chicken again" doesn't count. At this point, he couldn't think of more, which was again, a normal deficit in this brain injury I had to get used to for the time being. As a biologist, I think normally he could rattle off about sixty within the minute, but I needed to remind myself, and him, not to worry, that this will get better.

I remember one time I tied his shoelace up for him and he said, "how did you do that?" It was moments like this that reminded me of the sheer severity of his injury.

My heart went out to him. I knew he was serious; he was really asking me how to tie his shoes. He was really asking me how to read a schedule. He was really asking me how to tell time by looking at a clock. He really didn't remember speaking at his brother's memorial two years ago.

His motivation was inspiring. He was frustrated with some classes, he swore a lot, but he got through it. He was keen to learn, to do better, to walk, to come home. He was working his ass off, and I could see it every day. It was amazing, but it was also extremely difficult.

During this time, Kat and I remained close with Myp. We actually spent some time with both him and his wife, who was a nurse practitioner (right up Kat's alley). In addition to being an excellent doctor, Myp also had a wonderfully contagious personality. He knew when it was appropriate to laugh with us and be lighthearted, but he also knew when we needed a shoulder to lean on. He told us he was inspired by our care for our dad, and that he believed we were the reason Dad had made it through. He also mentioned that reading the thank you letter we wrote to him was one of the most impactful moments of his career. We felt so honored to know Myp.

Mom wasn't doing well. It was difficult to deal with because Dad always asked about her. He seemed to remember that she had a drinking problem but didn't remember how bad things had gotten, particularly in the past two years. Part of me wondered if maybe it was a good thing that he didn't remember, but another part of me grieved this loss of memory.

I realized that it was a huge loss for me; the silver lining of Mom's addiction was how close Kat, Dad, and I had become over the past fifteen years. I didn't want to have to re-explain it, I knew I couldn't do the experience justice. Even though I wanted to protect him, I did want him to remember everything we went through. Even though it's traumatic, I wanted his life to start making sense again. It felt too difficult for Kat and me to try to start from square one with him. I hoped he would remember on his own again one day. It was hard to know where to draw the line with the information I was giving him. I didn't want to be too graphic, but I also refused to lie.

If he asked me how she was, I would tell him she was unwell, but would conveniently leave out the part where she was so drunk that she couldn't walk, or so drunk that she was yelling at her eighty-one-year-old mother. If he asked me where she was, I told him she was getting some help with her mental health, rather than reminding him that she was currently creating chaos at our family home and that everyone was begging her to go to treatment. If he asked me if I saw her last night, I would tell him no and end it there rather than include the part where, even though I didn't see her, I was calling for another missing persons while she was later found hanging out with her twenty-year-old addict friend – a slumber party I suppose. If he asked me when she was coming, I would say, "hopefully soon" rather than reminding him how unpredictable her disease was and that there was no way of knowing when she would show up again.

What sucked the most was the feeling of not having a mom, even though she was still physically there in front of me. I've always had a hard time wrapping my head around that; she's there, but she's not really there. She's talking or moving, but she's not talking to me or moving in a direction I want.

Some days were good, and I caught glimpses of the mom I used to know. But then it's gone, and it's gone fast. The addict side is more present. During this time, the glimpses of her old self were becoming less and less frequent. It was like dangling candy in front of a baby; I wanted the relationship, but I just couldn't get it. I wanted her to be healthy, but I didn't know how much longer I could chase her. I was mentally and physically exhausted. I was so fucking tired.

We were told by professionals to draw a hard line; tell her she was out of our lives forever if she didn't get help. Kick her out, lock the doors, and change the locks. Easier said than done. You tell me how I'm supposed to say that to someone with a fifty-fifty chance of them becoming unstable and committing suicide. Then that's on me. How do you draw a hard line when you're constantly toying with death?

How do I walk away from her if that might be the last time I see her? How do I say something aggressive—because I'm so fucking mad—knowing it might tip her over the edge and that will have been the last thing I ever said to her? How do I go to bed at night knowing she's not home and it's been six hours and I don't know where she is, or if she's alive? How do I make the decision to call the cops and arrange a search party? How do I draw a hard line?

I was still trying to figure it out while Dad was in recovery. I'd been harsh with her, but maybe not harsh enough. I didn't know how much worse it could get; it was getting physical, and I couldn't figure out how to feel about it. I couldn't stay up until two a.m. waiting for her to come home just so I could go to bed knowing she was breathing.

I thought we were done with this life. I couldn't force her to recover. I refused to continue the way we were going. I was twenty-five, I felt like an animal chasing my tail and I needed to stop. I needed to get away from it. But I couldn't stray too far because she might have a crisis and need me. That's where I drew the line at that point: no relationship outside of needing me in a crisis or emergency. Done.

My main pain was knowing that Dad was coming home to this chaos in two months. I wouldn't allow it. It was bad enough for him here when he was healthy, but he now had an injury from which he would likely be recovering for his whole life, and stress was likely going to halt that process.

I decided that I would get us an apartment if Mom was still in a bad place when it was time for him to be discharged. I would not allow him to be around the toxic relapses. I would work hard to protect him, like he did for us. I hated that I had to protect him from his own wife, my mother, but until she was healthy, it was the only path to take. Quite frankly, she is not his wife or my mother when she is using. She is the addict, and not someone we want to be around at this point. We want Mom back, but it's too risky to accept any less.

I could not put into words how clear it became that as much agony as addiction and loss had brought this family, it was incomparable to the heartache I felt at the thought of losing my dad. Even though we didn't lose him, it was still incredibly painful to not have him at one hundred percent. It was still painful seeing the strongest, most amazing man I know go through such a challenging situation.

It goes to show how numb I was about my mom's addiction; for years, I had worried myself sick about losing her, but the pain of witnessing her addiction made me now feel numb to the thought. I knew it would still be devastating, but I was numb.

What else could possibly go wrong?

COVID-19

Of course. A fucking virus. A virus that became a global pandemic. We had to be separated from Dad so that we could all remain safe and healthy, and to prevent the virus from spreading further. I completely agreed with the health measures needed to keep everyone safe, but it was painful to be separated after not missing a beat of his recovery so far. I knew I was going to miss him exclaiming "There's one of my girls!" as soon as Kat or I walked in his room.

We bought him an iPad so we could FaceTime every day. I would FaceTime him almost all day on weekends because I knew he had nothing to do; no classes, no programs, fewer staff. I couldn't stand him being lonely, it hurt me deeper than I could bear, so I would stay on FaceTime with him until he was ready to go to bed or go to class during the week. Sometimes we just sat on FaceTime in silence and did our own things, just so he would have the feeling that someone else was in the room with him.

He only had one month left. Unfortunately, it was a month without visiting. I thought about family members who were at the beginning of their loved ones' injuries, down at VGH in the ER or the ICU. I couldn't imagine being separated from my dad that early on, with restricted visiting hours. It would be unbearable. I was grateful that we only had a month left.

Well, it was a harder month than I thought. I just didn't realize how much we were doing there until we left. Who was doing his laundry now? Who would buy him new pants and socks? Who was going to bring up issues to the nurse and get them sorted? Who was going to adjust his schedule on the white board every Friday for the upcoming week? Who was going to help him move rooms when VGH sent patients to GF Strong to make more room? Who was going to just sit there and be with him?

It killed me that we could no longer do any of these things. It was an indescribably frustrating feeling for me when I wanted to fix something but couldn't. One day he mentioned that his bathroom buddy (patients may have their own room but the bathroom is often shared with the patient in the next room) was a jerk to him and that was enough to make me want to march right over there and give the guy a piece of my mind. I hated dealing with that mental anxiety from a distance.

I was beyond grateful for Brittany, his OT. She updated me a lot, texted me videos, kept me in the loop, and really worked hard to help us out. She even moved his room for him; she packed up all his stuff, moved it, unpacked it, and redecorated the new room exactly like his old one. That was something Kat and I would have done, and it melted my heart that she was selflessly filling those shoes when we were unable to.

There were good moments, but the reality was that everything was happening at once, and the pandemic wasn't making anything easier. This is what a typical day in my life looked like during that time:

It's Monday. This fine morning consists of Dad being upset about his GF Strong bathroom buddy. We're not there to help so I have to text my OT friend. Mom is threatening to call the cops on us because we have her wallet—don't even get me started. Dad is hearing about this which results in him being upset and worried, which doesn't help the brain healing process, of course. A client is yelling at me on the phone—yes,

I'm still helplessly trying to keep my job. I'm getting groceries because I'm out of food and can't have pesto pasta for the third night in a row, and I'm coming back to the suite to find the roof leaking—great. I'm getting a call from the bike shop guy to pick up my fixed bike before the store closes in two hours. I'm talking on the phone with a GF Strong doctor while trying to write an email to the PT. Grandma is needing the laurel cut. I'm having one of many three-way calls with Aunty Jacquie—Mom's sister—and Kat to figure out the next steps for Mom. I'm getting off that call because Dad's trying to FaceTime me. I'm getting a call from our family doctor who is unaware of Dad's accident or Mom's addiction – is there a short version I can give her? I'm trying to fit in a workout but being cut short due to another call with my sister and older cousin, about Mom, of course. I'm heading out again to get ant killer because I can't pee with them crawling up my legs again. It's three in the afternoon and I have a meeting in ninety minutes for work. Guess I better cancel that FaceTime call with my friends. Oh shit, the bike.

It's not right that by the afternoon I already have too much cortisol in my body. I feel like I'm vibrating. Maybe I should just go to bed and try again at life tomorrow.

Just kidding—Mom's acting up again. She's living at our house on the Sunshine Coast, because she left treatment AMA and refused to go back. This is dangerous because she's alone in the house, and we all know what happens when she's alone. She's drinking day-in and day-out. She's falling. She's having fires inside in the heat of August. She's out of control. My aunt and uncle are checking in on her to try to avoid our worst fear: death. My sister and I need to stay with Dad. It's gotten so bad we've had to cut off communication her with for a bit, because this is completely unmanageable.

Only a few days into no communication, she sends Kat a picture of blood in the toilet. This is the type of manipulation that addicts tend to pull. As we're trying to create solid healthy boundaries, we're constantly having to break them down because, as I said before, if she's going to threaten suicide or anything along those lines, we have no choice. So now we have to communicate with her because she clearly has a GI bleed and might die from that, and death is the thing we are constantly trying to avoid. Well-played Mom, well-played.

If I had a dime for every hour I put into trying to get her better—well, let's just say I'd stop buying lottery tickets.

So, we decide we need the cops involved yet again, only this time, they can't take her away against her will when she's not admitting she's suicidal. We need something stronger. We need a warrant.

So, Kat spends hours, which turned into days and weeks, writing a letter and working with a judge to get a warrant to take Mom to the psych unit at St. Mary's hospital on the Sunshine Coast.

Finally, we get it. After all the times she has left the hospital AMA, we now have the solution: a warrant and certification. My heart breaks a little bit thinking of her being taken away from her own house in handcuffs, but this is the only way she will survive, and I have to keep reminding myself of that. We had been begging doctors to certify her for months, but they would all say the same thing: that it was against her human rights to keep her against her own will. So, I guess when she's dead we'll just say, "At least we let her keep her human rights though!" What a joke.

Finally, we could breathe. She is certified for thirty days. That means thirty days of total focus on Dad, thirty days of sleep, thirty days of not calling 911 —maybe they will forget my first name now—thirty days to let my blood pressure come down.

But you know my mom well enough by this point, don't you? She can sweet talk her way out of just about anything. Because she was in the healthcare field, she knew exactly what to say to get her out of there. All she had to do was tell them she was not feeling suicidal anymore, was feeling much better, and wanted a reassessment. Not many people know you can do this, but by law, a psychiatrist must come reassess her, and if she doesn't present as a risk to her own life in that moment, they must let her go. Amazing, isn't it?

I remember talking to the psychiatrist on the phone, desperately trying to understand how she could possibly be on her way back home in less than eight hours. He explained to me that once he reassesses her, and she presents well, he's in for a lawsuit if she takes it to court and he's kept her.

But have you looked at her history? She's in here like once a week, and every time she is lucky to be alive. So I guess we'll just see you next week when she's back? Then what? Certified again? Reassessed and heading out again?

It's not the doctor's fault—it's our system. Our system fails us miserably on the mental health spectrum, because honest to god, how the hell could it even be possible for someone to UN-certify themselves. Isn't that illegal? Only Mom could accomplish something like this. That addict brain can be so incredibly brilliant.

And when she comes home, boy is she mad at us for having gotten that warrant. She claims it's humiliating to be taken out of her house like that, and that we were bullying her. She feels we haven't dealt with her addiction correctly. Well, if there's a rule book to addiction I haven't found yet, please send it my way and I'd be more than happy to take a look. My mind can't comprehend this. We also saved your life? Over and over and over again. "You're welcome" is my only comment.

I compare this to my dad's injury a lot, in terms of the help. Dad suffers a severe head injury and is taken to the top trauma hospital in the province—maybe even the country—and he is taken care of by world-renowned ICU doctors and surgeons. Millions of dollars are spent to keep him alive. Every decision they make with him is carefully thought out. They keep track of all his vitals hourly. They are doing everything they can, and they are always planning one step ahead of themselves. They make sure his best interest is always top of mind.

I witnessed this care, this incredible system that saved his life. I think about our mental health system, and it's devastating how poor it is, in comparison. When Mom uses, the first step is to take her to detox, but at least half the times we call, they are full. We've had the same encounters with treatment, sometimes their beds are just simply full and there's no room for her. How can we have a system in which someone who finally accepts they are sick, finally accepts they aren't currently beating this addiction, finally accepts the help, is told no? How can it be that we call the cops, but they aren't able to take her away unless she verbally admits she's suicidal AND has a plan to kill herself? Can you not take our word for it?

She can't say it now because she's too drunk to speak, or because she's figured out if she admits it, she will be taken back to the psych unit. How can we have a system in which there are no other ways to keep her safe than to handcuff her, take her out of the house, into the police car, to the hospital, and certify her? Why is she able to get 'reassessed' within hours of being there, and let go upon knowing the system and purposely acting normal? Look back in the chart, man! She was considered psychotic three hours ago and this is a repeated pattern. Like I said, if you don't keep her, we'll be back next week, and this time she might not make it.

How can it be that treatment is unaffordable for most families, most centers are thousands of dollars per month (i.e. the most frequent one we took her to was $8200/month)—if that's not a deterrent for the addict, I don't know what is. How can there possibly be a world in which the only way to get an addict sober is to have THEM make the decision? We're putting this in THEIR HANDS? I understand they ultimately need to want it, but what if they are too sick to make that good decision to go get help? Can they make that choice? What the fuck do we do at that point?

How it is possible that even if an addict does get sober, they still struggle to be treated equally in society? I imagine it's hard to stay sober when there are so many barriers in place threatening to push you off track. All we do if we don't include them in our communities is punish them for their past, a past they didn't ask for, a past they are incredibly shameful of, and a past they are working hard to overcome.

Our system is broken. Our system is failing us.

I don't blame detox or treatment centers. I don't blame the cops or doctors or psychiatrists; their hands are tied in what they are able to legally do. It's not their fault. But something needs to change.

There needs to first be more understanding of and education for addiction. I say above that I don't blame doctors. Let's be clear that I am referring to the doctors that have been very empathetic and done everything they can for mom while staying within the law. We have worked with wonderful, caring, thoughtful, and empathic physicians. For doctors that seem to have less patience for addiction, or worse, carry a large judgement of it in their day-to-day work, these are the ones that need some education. We've experienced the way some doctors look at mom. We've experienced her receive less care because of why she is there. We've experienced the stigma and judgment. We've experienced having to fight harder for her because we're fighting against a doctors' pre-conceived idea that she is beyond help, or worse, undeserving. I suppose this is just simply unaware, naive, and un-educated individuals on the disease of addiction. I'm sure if it were their loved one, they would have a very different outlook. One doctor actually said to Kat "well, she's an alcoholic, she's going to die at some point", as if this was an easy excuse to not provide care to her. This was heartbreaking to hear, especially from a medical professional who should know better. She is sick. She is suffering. She is deserving of healthcare. She has a family who is desperately hoping she will come back to them one day and creating more stigma in healthcare is only a barrier to that hope. Every healthcare professional should be looking at these patients as if it were their loved one. They should be full of compassion wondering why this patient is in so much pain that they need to use drugs. They should be curious rather than angry. They should have the knowledge of thoughtful intervention for any addict that walks through their doors. The addict may refuse help, but at the very least it needs to be offered. There needs to be more education and less stigma. Period.

There needs to be more government funding for detox facilities and treatment centers. This could potentially bring down costs so that finances are not a barrier to getting help. This would also provide more beds and space so that no addict that finally accepts help is turned away. They will die if they are turned away. They may die anyways, but how disgraceful to die the one time they tried. This is unacceptable.

There needs to be more options for those unwilling to do long-term inpatient residential treatment, but that are willing to do more than just NA/AA meetings and step-work. I feel there could be something developed that lands somewhere in the middle. Maybe this looks like shorter term outpatient programs that focus on developing skills to cope with pain and improve quality of life, through both 1:1 and group work with therapists specializing in addictions treatment. Breaking this down: short term may cost less and feel less daunting which would increase motivation, outpatient would remove the feeling of permanency, 1:1 work would target overcoming individualized pain, group work would reduce feelings of isolation (as mom says from her meetings, "the opposite of addiction is connection"), qualified therapists would provide meaningful education, and coping and improving quality of life would lessen the chance of utilizing the drug for those very purposes.

In terms of harder drugs, the answer may lie in decriminalizing them, and then using a harm reduction approach. I realize it sounds ironic—how could we possibly say that now the government is going to be the dealer. Yes, but they are the safe dealer. If we can regulate the sales and/or usage of drugs, we can save lives. People are dying, not necessarily because of taking too much of a drug, but because they are unknowingly taking drugs that are toxically laced—with Fentanyl, for example—and dying within minutes. We need to create more space for safe injection sites, and safe drug supplies.

If you're still not convinced, compare this to alcohol. The selling of alcohol was forbidden in the early 1900s, and alcohol-related deaths were very high. As soon as they decriminalized it, the death rate went down significantly [2]. Yes, people still die from alcoholism of course, but allowing the legal selling of it did have a huge impact.

Why shouldn't we do the same with drugs? Wouldn't you expect to see a reduction in overdose-related deaths? Addicts will use, and if they don't have the drug, they WILL find a way to get it. Keeping drugs illegal will only put them at risk for dying when they take their drugs. If we accept that they are going to use, but allow them to use a safe supply, we not only save lives, but we extend the time they have to get to the point of potentially making the decision to go get clean. Not to mention, violence would likely be reduced as a result; why would the addict feel the need to do whatever it takes, even if that means harming others, to get the pain-numbing drug if it's already available to them when they want it? They wouldn't. The addict gets their regulated drug, they have a chance at potential recovery with continued community support, less violence occurs and as a result, people feel safer. Everybody wins.

And people still believe COVID-19 was the crisis... the overdose scene has been going on for a long, long time. This is our real crisis.

I know we have come a long way. The NA/AA meetings are incredible. There are very influential and inspiring people working their recovery. You can go out and get a sponsor, work the steps, attend meetings, and work on sobriety. And although this is great, not every addict has the supports in place to get to a meeting, or they are too sick to feel motivated to get the help. This is where we need more help in our system. Make it match our medical system. Mental health is just as important as physical health.

These addicts are good people. It's easy to look at them and think they deserve the situation they are in, they asked for this, they are choosing not to get out of this rut they are in. I say this because this *was me* before I had experienced addiction so close to me. Remember, this could just have easily been YOU. You could have had the genetic and/or environmental conditions that forced you into addiction and changed your life forever.

You think you're better than this? You're not. Let's review my mom's trajectory of a successful, well-known, very well-loved community nurse and incredible mother...she fell into addiction. As I've mentioned, from cloud nine to addiction. It can happen to anyone. I hope you remember that the next time you drive down Vancouver's downtown east side – when you see these individuals, remember they are not that different from you. They are human, just like you, that had the unfortunate circumstances that landed them here; verbal, sexual, or physical abuse, neglect, pain, trauma, mental health illnesses, poverty, homelessness, unemployment... the list goes on. And the horror stories they've lived through are likely a huge factor playing a role in *why* they use... wouldn't you use a drug if it was the only thing that could numb the pain and help you forget an upbringing of horrendous sexual assaults? If you still don't buy it, ask yourself *why would anyone choose that life?* No one would choose that life. They didn't choose that life, so stop acting like they did. Don't feel disgust, feel privilege. Feel grateful. Feel lucky that this isn't you, because if it was, I'm sure you would pray that people wouldn't judge why or how you got there or decide who you are as a person based on what they see, the clothes on your body or the shoes on your feet. Let's act like addiction has hurt all of us, let's have sympathy for those suffering from it. I repeat, sometimes they can act like assholes, but they are suffering, trust me, and that is desperation and trauma speaking. So, let's get them the help they need. Let's see who they really are beneath this addiction, because I bet you'll like them without their addiction. I bet you'll like them a lot.

Addicts don't recover from their mental illness overnight. I think we all know that.

Dammit, the roof is leaking again. And we have more ants in the bathroom. Because why not?

This is the first year for a long time I didn't prank someone for April Fools'. I guess life felt like enough of a joke.

My counsellor, Noa, helped me figure out the necessities versus the things that can wait. Extra work obligations, friends, and unfortunately Mom are on the back burner for now. Dad, helping Grandma, and basic work tasks that help me keep my job are the priorities. This is because I can't manage it all; something has to give. So, although my extra work tasks, friends, and Mom are highly important to me, they are things that need to take the hit for now. Mom is continuing to resist the support anyways, so I need to stop trying harder than she is to get her into sobriety.

I hate feeling like I'm not doing as well as I could in my career. I worked so hard to get to where I am. I love my job. I work as an outpatient Dietitian in a clinic with interdisciplinary others. I help clients feel empowered in their food choices. I help them optimize their health through nutrition. I see everything from cholesterol management to diabetes to plant-based diets to inflammation to gut health to pregnancy to sport nutrition, the list goes on. It's exciting to be in an environment where I'll always be learning. I was so keen all through school to get a job like this. I was so invested at the start; I love the team, I love the work, how lucky. I put so much time and effort into everything I did there.

When Dad first got hurt, they gave me some time off. I was grateful for this. Eventually I started working part-time again, as I was told by Dad's doctors that this was a long recovery and I needed to try to have some normalcy again. They estimated eight months before having a solid understanding of what his future would look like. Although I decided not to believe this absurd news at first, I understood as days went by how very long this recovery was going to be, if at all possible. So, I tried going back part-time. It seemed like a good distraction. But I could tell I wasn't one hundred percent there. I would see clients, but I was just thinking about any improvements in Dad I might be missing that day, or whether Mom was still sober that day.

I feel like I'm so anxious that I'm getting that brain fog thing again; sometimes I forget the client's question as I'm in the middle of answering it, and I need to try to find my way to the end of the sentence in a way that makes sense and doesn't allow them to know that I forgot the question. It's embarrassing. I get nervous for things I never used to get nervous for, like Zoom meetings or friend hangouts. It's ridiculous.

Noa explains it so well—"look at what you've been through with your parents, mostly your mom. Trauma after trauma, threat after threat. So now your brain is on autopilot— it will prepare for a threat even in situations where there is little to no chance of a threat."

How sad. I've gotten to a point where my body is stuck in this fight or flight response, where I'm shaking and sweating for simple things that would never result in a threat. I need therapy more than ever. I need to heal what has been so viciously damaged. I want my old self back.

DISCHARGE DAY

The GF Strong discharge date finally arrived. It wasn't quite how we envisioned it. We had planned to say goodbye to everyone there, then drop by VGH and have Dad meet the doctors who saved his life, but we knew that would have to wait until this global crisis had settled. We said our goodbyes, which was more emotional than I had anticipated, both for us and for the staff, who all fell in love with Dad. This team became family to us and supported us through the last three months in this rehab center. After impatiently counting down the days to take Dad home, I was suddenly caught off guard with sadness when it came time to leave. Again, bittersweet. We gathered everything from his room and drove to my grandma's house in North Vancouver to isolate there.

This part was harder than I had anticipated. There was a lot to do: start making him three meals per day plus snacks, ensure he took his daily medications (luckily he had weaned down to just one anti-epileptic drug: lacosamide, that would likely be life-long to prevent any future seizures), get the place set up for his needs, get drawers for his room, acquire the equipment necessary for his continued at-home rehab, complete all his physical therapy exercises together, get in touch with DFO to go through sick time and disability protocols, figure out taxes because it was February, and the hardest part—reteach him the skills he needed to function normally again.

Not only was he still learning how to walk and talk, but he needed to learn how to make food, get gas, use a credit or debit card, reset all his bank PINs for his cards because he didn't remember his old ones, and much more.

Of course, I had to bring him into the bank for proof of his injury, you know how banks are. Luckily, after explaining our story, the bank teller changed his POA from my mom to me, and Dad signed off on it. This wasn't easy but we managed to separate the financial accounts enough to feel a bit more at ease if she remained unwell and unintentionally drained them. She was angry that I was dealing with her finances now, but I also couldn't leave Dad with nothing. I didn't want to be this involved in their money, but there was no longer any choice. She was unpredictable, and Dad voiced that he needed the reassurance that he did still have some savings for the future. We still didn't know what the long-term plan was for work and disability, so we needed to plan for the worst. If she had been there to be his caregiver, I would never have had to get in the middle of things.

We walked out of the bank feeling a bit more empowered than when we walked in, except for when I got into my car and realized I had a ticket for being parked thirty minutes over the limit. Dammit.

He had numerous appointments every week, usually consisting of PT, OT, speech, and neurologist visits. I was always present for these appointments, taking notes and making sure I understood the plan incase Dad forgot or confused it. I would get caught in a feeling of guilt as they would ask how certain aspects of his recovery were going: balance, hand function, memory, temperament, etcetera. Dad would usually report they were fine, which wasn't entirely accurate at this point. I don't think he was intentionally being dishonest, but rather hopeful and not wanting to be told to slow down. I couldn't lie to the neurologist so I would say the truth: balance isn't good, he's falling when trying to run or do stairs, memory is very weak, and temperament fluctuates. I would feel bad as they took notes and Dad sat in silence. These are the things he doesn't want to hear.

"It's just so that they can get an accurate picture of your recovery so they can do everything they can to help you" I would say.

"I know, sweetie."

Now it was time for the part I was most worried about: Dad was home, and Mom wasn't in treatment. She was going to want to see him.

Unfortunately, she drank on his discharge date. He had his hopes up because she had been sober for one week, and this day was important—it was a milestone for him. She missed another important event. I felt more heartbroken for him than myself. Addiction really does destroy families.

I continued to worry about the long-term effects of stress on my health, and my family's health, after facing this addiction for so long.

I went to the dentist and the hygienist was saying I have "fragile tissue type gums." I had never heard this before. It came as a shock because I take good care of my teeth and the dentist always says I'm doing a great job. I've always been proud of my oral hygiene, actually. So much so that I would look forward to seeing the dentist just so my Type A personality could get the annual "you have great teeth" stamp of approval. She mentioned it could be a result of inflammation, from chronic stress. Bingo. Now I'm having the risk of periodontal disease from this stress? Great.

I often found myself looking in the mirror and doing the FAST acronym—face, arms, speech, time—to ensure I wasn't having a stroke. I had nights where I was almost asleep and it hit: sweating, heart racing, mind scattered. Hot flashes came over me like waves, leading me to question if I was going through menopause twenty-five years too early. I would feel my face to make sure it was still even.

My chest hurt and my heart was pounding, which made me wonder if I was having a heart attack. I knew I was too young for either a stroke or a heart attack, but I also knew how powerful the effects of stress could be on the body, and part of me believed it was possible.

The thought of the possibility made the heat waves come more often and last longer. I questioned if I should wake my dad up and tell him how I was feeling. I even sometimes questioned calling an ambulance; I knew when it came to strokes, your recovery depends on how fast you treat them.

I can't explain the fear of these episodes. I had never felt so out of control in my entire life. I had never experienced anything like it. Panic attacks. I can't believe I once thought they weren't real.

When is she coming? Should she be here? How will I lock the door? How will I keep her from Dad? Or should I? Is Dad safe? I'm scared. Fuck, it's one thirty a.m.

I couldn't shake my anxiety about how Mom was going to handle Dad's ongoing need for care and support. One day, she came to my grandma's house to visit him, and I will never forget how my body and mind naturally responded.

I was outside doing some business work and Dad was lying down in his room. Mom went to go lie beside him and talk. I found myself subconsciously doing things to keep engaged in what was happening in that room. I was trying to read my computer screen, but I kept the door open and one earphone out of my ear in case anything happened.

After a few minutes, I realized there was silence; no more conversation coming from the room. My lack of trust in her, and the reality of knowing how difficult this situation was for her, made me convinced something bad was happening within those walls.

My brain convinced me that the silence meant he wasn't breathing, and that she was behind it. I had a panic attack imagining she was suffocating him, to put this past her and get rid of the constant pain that she couldn't handle. I ran down the hallway and burst open the door only to see the two of them lying there looking out the window. They both jumped when I came in and asked what was going on. I managed to get out, "Ahh, I was just wondering if you wanted a snack, Dad. You haven't eaten since lunch." He said he was fine, and out I walked.

What the fuck is wrong with me?

It's amazing what our brains will convince ourselves of when we have past trauma. I was convinced I would run in to that room having it be too late and him gone, and her having done something she would regret for the rest of her life, her actions having been a consequence of her own trauma and mental state.

But that wasn't the case at all. Our brains do work with anxiety, but they also work with what they've known in the past. Clearly, she had given my brain a reason to believe that, although it's crazy, it's not impossible. She would never do something like that in her right mind, but what she would do while using felt like a gamble.

While we were still getting the house set up for Dad, Mom was taken to the ER at VGH, with talk of liver failure. Kat brought up the idea of liver donation, if one of us matched her blood type. I couldn't even believe we were having this conversation, but we both agreed that, if they time came, we would get tested and help however we could.

Apparently her liver was fatty, but not yet cirrhotic. I had never met someone who had done so much damage to their liver while still being in a reversible stage. God bless you, Whooee, and your resilient genes.

Back to detox—but detox flooded because it was raining so much. Of course. Just another clear sign we need more funding for these facilities. So back home it is—cheers.

LIVING WITH ADDICTION &
TRAUMATIC BRAIN INJURY

It became extremely difficult to manage the mindfuck of Dad not remembering how bad Mom's addiction was; he always seemed to be 'siding' with her, for lack of a better term. He used to have our backs no matter what because he knew the addiction inside and out, but the result of this injury made him confused when I would remind him to take caution with Mom.

He sometimes said, "just go easy on her." He would have ripped someone's head off if they had said that to him eight months prior. It's so easy to look at the picture of addiction and say, "just do (blank)" or agree that a family should be nicer, calmer, more patient, or stronger. But until you are fully immersed in addiction, you don't get to say that. It's much more complex than it looks from the outside.

I felt sick to my stomach knowing this was our reality, that he didn't know what we were talking about with the depth of her history. I didn't even know where to start. Would he even believe me? How could I explain without it looking like I had it out for her, and that I'm only protecting him?

How do I do it? Why do I have to do it? We used to joke about one of us forgetting, how hard it would be to explain. Even when Dad was in the hospital, we used to joke about how ironic it would be if he woke up and forgot Mom's past. I never thought my fears would become my reality. It was only funny before because it was *just a joke.*

When he would back her up or take her side, there were no words to describe how betrayed I felt. I knew he didn't feel like he was betraying me; he didn't remember her terrible behavior with this addiction, and she was sneaky enough to hide it from him after his injury, so I really couldn't blame him. I just needed him to put it together; Kat and I were the ones who had been there for him from the beginning of his injury. We were by his bedside every single day, holding his hand, making him music playlists, telling him stories, going to team rounds, taking part in his care, missing work and school to be there for him. All the while, mom was drinking and was too sick to be there. He did not get to take her side after this. He needed to trust us and be on our side no matter what. He is the one I trust, look up to, and admire. I don't want to change the way I look at him.

I will never forget the blowout we had at Grandma's one day. Mom was not in her right mind and therefore was manipulating me all day. She was whispering things so only I could hear them, waiting for me to lose it and then have Dad see that I "wasn't being nice to her."

She did this all day until I finally did lose it. I freaked out and when Dad told me to just calm down, I replied, "why don't you tell that to your *fucking wife*" and slammed the door on him. So then of course he lost it. He was so angry, he was yelling. But he was yelling at me. This was now his brain injury talking, not him. He was on autopilot. I will never get the "fuck you, you fucking asshole" out of my head, banging his left elbow against my bedroom door, over and over and over again, his face red as a tomato. He looked like he could seriously hurt me, although I knew he wouldn't. This was the kind of trauma and distrust we had with Mom; I didn't need it with two parents. Well, you won that one, Mom.

I left to go to Kat's for a week. The first day I was away, Dad tried Facetiming me eleven times. I ignored all of them. And again and again for two days after.

He was trying. He talked to his sister; he knows he fucked up. He said, "just tell her to come home, I need her, please tell her to come back, I can't do this without her" over and over and over again. This shattered my heart—but he learned a valuable lesson. He couldn't do this without me, not yet. And he couldn't back Mom up over me ever again.

I was also hurt by the fact that Mom had stopped trying with me. Yes, I finally told her I felt done, but that shouldn't stop her from trying to make amends with her own daughter. Her addict brain convinced her that no matter how much she abused us under the influence of drugs, we would still always be there.

She didn't reach out once; no call, text, email, nothing. That's the difference between a sick and a healthy brain: Dad was trying, Dad was not giving up, Dad was calling me again and again until I picked up because he knew he screwed up. He was willing to admit it, apologize, do whatever I needed to help us move forward, and he knew it was up to him to make that happen.

I am all for forgiveness when there's accountability. Mom was too damn proud to give me the time of day. What's fucked up is that Dad didn't actually have a "healthy" brain then either, but he still knew the right thing to do, he still knew right from wrong. That's why, although I knew it was due to sickness, it was hard to accept this behaviour with mom.

It looked like Mom was going to die. I had grieved her death so many times I'd lost count. I begrudgingly accepted it a long time ago because I lost her a long time ago. It has been so exhausting that I have wondered if life would just be easier without her—and let me honestly tell you, I feel sick for even wondering that. The sad thing is that I've been grieving losing her since I was fifteen years old.

It's August 2020, and we're spending this lovely Monday convincing her to go to treatment. She's on the coast. We're at my grandma's in North Vancouver.

Mom refuses to go to treatment. She claims she will be going to her nurse practitioner appointment in Vancouver on Thursday. Okay well we have to MAKE IT to Thursday first…

"You won't live another two weeks", were the exact words from the nurse practitioner's mouth.

Mom still isn't convinced.

Kat brings her to meet us at Grandmas'. As soon as we beg her to go to treatment, she demands more of the drug to comply. We adhere because we are that desperate for her to go. Manipulation at its finest.

We end up spending that Thursday begging her to go to treatment—am I still doing this?—reminding her that if she heads back to the coast, she will die, that this will be the last time we see her. It takes HOURS to get her to say "maybe."

I end up getting the rest of the day off work because THIS is a full-time job—that I don't get paid for and that comes with really shitty benefits, wondering how many "sick days" I have left. She asks for a brief intermission from this intervention to go pee. Fine, I guess I won't stop you from your bodily functions needing attention. She spends a bit too long in there—classic red flag—and she comes out hammered. I go in after her and she's got a two-six in there with her that she was stashing in the toilet tank. Of course.

How the fuck did that happen? She came STRAIGHT from the coast where her backpack was searched by a family member, onto the ferry—where there's no booze sold the last time I checked—to Horseshoe Bay at seven in the morning—when nothing is open the last time I checked—straight into Kat's car, and Kat drove her to her appointment, and then straight to grandmas. My brain cannot understand how the hell she got a hold of this, and when. God dammit she is a magician if I ever met one.

Now she's drunk, so she's mean again and belligerent. Now she's refusing treatment again, so the last five hours of getting to that "maybe" have gone to shit.

She demands more alcohol so that she can avoid the painful withdrawal. We say no because she isn't going through withdrawal yet. She begs. We say no. She reminds us she could have a seizure if she goes through withdrawal. We remind her that she isn't possibly going through withdrawal yet if she just chugged half a two-six. She threatens not going to treatment. Well, you got us there, don't you, Mom. She knows that's our weak spot because we are desperate for her to go. Again, manipulation at its finest.

Luckily, counselling is teaching me to see beyond her words, to see the pain, guilt, shame, and suffering underneath.

We physically have to feed her a bit of alcohol to keep her in that range of being drunk enough that she's not going to go through withdrawal and not refusing to get help, but not so drunk that she can't stand up and won't be accepted at the treatment center. It's a fine line. And it's a disgusting thing to have to pour out measured amounts of vodka for someone you love.

I can feel her eyes on me, watching as I pour it. I look to meet her gaze, and I can see the desperation in her eyes. I can barely finish pouring before she's snatched it from the counter and forcefully thrown it down her throat. I have never seen her eyes locked on something so intensely in my life. And these are the moments I never forget. I will never forget that look. It was like the look from a vicious dog when you are cutting roast beef and dangling it in front of its face. I can't shake that off. I would have flashbacks of the words of wisdom she would bring back from her meetings: "one is too many, and one thousand is never enough." Ain't that the truth.

After eight hours of discussion, she decides she's leaving for the coast. I tell her that she'll die if she goes home, but that's her call. She glares at me as she throws on her jacket. Kat begs her to go to treatment. But she puts her backpack on and ties her shoes anyways.

It's not until Dad says, "If you walk out that door, I'll never see you again, and you can mail me the divorce papers to sign." Finally, he threatened divorce. We all know he's bluffing, and he's been terrified to say this, but it's the only thing she might listen to. And she does. She slowly slides her backpack off her back, turns around, and sits back down. I guess she does have enough healthy brain cells to realize a broken marriage is not what she wants right now. They are both still stubbornly devoted to their marriage. I didn't think there would ever be a "D" word a person would fear more than death, but here we are. Take your coat off, have a seat, stay a while...

So, after ten hours, she's in treatment. Thank the fucking lord. I'm going to get a good sleep tonight.

REHAB

After Mom went to treatment, Dad and I moved back to the coast. It was incredible to see his memory come back so much just from being there.

When he first woke up, he didn't remember ever playing rugby or soccer, or even coaching, when he had spent most of his life doing both. He was arguably the soccer league's finest player, and his athletic ability for his age was spoken of very highly among his peers, being well known for his diving goal-scoring headers, despite having one eye. He was frequently referred to as 'fancy feet' or 'twinkle toes', as he could quite easily maneuver the ball around the opposition, often moving too quickly to be effectively checked. After one week of being on the coast and around the soccer fields, it started coming back to him. One day he said, "I remember, you were center midfield, just like me." Since soccer was a big thing he started to remember, and something that made him happy, I tried to make it a larger part of his life. I would tell him where and when my Sunday league games were, and he would never fail to show up to watch. We would go watch the U18 boys' games together on Saturdays. He even came to my Wednesday night drop ins – we had a routine of going to IGA first to get food and apple juice, his favorite, and he would then sit on the sidelines eating dinner while he watched a scrimmage. He used to play in a Squamish tournament every year called the Squamish Soccerfest, and I can remember watching the games all weekend with my mom and Kat, even when we were just little kids. I was lucky enough to be asked to play in the Squamish tournament this year and Dad was excited to come watch. What a role reversal, but an incredibly exciting one.

Being back home was a great feeling after being gone for a whole year. It was so nice to live in the place where I grew up, especially compared to the hospital. And the support continued to be overwhelming. We saw familiar faces every time we got groceries at IGA or dropped off recycling at the depot. The owners of IGA, Bob and Sue Hoy, had been incredible supports to our family, so it was great to start seeing them regularly again. We had rugby, soccer, and family friends reaching out constantly to offer to make food, trim the yard, or drop off firewood. We had a wonderful family friend, Sandra Kern, who's also the mom of one of my best friends, give our bedrooms a makeover: new bed sheets, duvets, pillows, and even shams! I didn't even know what shams were before this. She owns a furniture store on the coast, and my god she is a generous human.

I made a Facebook post asking where Dad and I could buy a used stationary bike so he could get some cardio indoors during the winter months when it's too slippery to do his hills. I had comments within seconds from old rugby friends all offering to pitch in one hundred dollars each and buy him a new one.

I couldn't believe it. We didn't want people to buy us one, of course, we just wanted to know where *we* could buy one! Two days later we had a used bike from a family friend show up in the driveway. Just incredible.

Every day I saw something in Dad that was hard to cope with. It wasn't his fault; it was just the situation. He might have said something he had never said before or been unable to help me with something he would have been able to do prior. He sometimes needed help to think of the words he was trying to say. He was often frustrated because he couldn't go for a bike ride like he used to, or drive to the store, or chop firewood outside. His body just wasn't functioning as he once knew it.

So, it was challenging for him, but it was also extremely challenging for me. I had to learn coping strategies when I saw something that reminded me of how severe his accident really was, to remind me that he still had a lot of work ahead of him before he got back to where he was… if he could ever get there.

I also needed to manage my anger with the situation. I felt angry that it ever happened to him. I got caught with my frustrations and wanted to scream into a pillow. I needed to control my emotions, because me getting mad didn't help anything. In fact, it made things worse, because I felt guilty for getting angry with him over things he couldn't control.

The mental health was one part of it, but the physical demands were another. Getting him ready for the grocery store, explaining how to find a recipe online, finding one together, making a list together, explaining how to walk through the store as we went, supporting the process of paying at the till, driving home only to move onto teaching him how to submit the claim from physio from that week, working on disability forms together (the bane of my god damn existence), calling the bank when we were locked out of the account and having them question why I was talking on his behalf (UGH!), calling Telus when the TV wasn't working. I could have done all these things in seconds myself (and so could he, before), but I knew in my heart that if I didn't take the time to show him, explain to him, and let him try, then I was failing him. I was putting up a barrier to success with the selfishness of trying to get things done faster, and at the cost of his recovery. I knew that wasn't fair to him. My goal was to have him be independent, to not rely on anyone, to be able to go back to work if he so desired. I knew the only way I could do this was to push him. Push him, but support him. I would make him call the bank, but they were on speaker phone and I was right beside him if anything went sideways. I would get him to make the grocery list, but I always made my own too, in case his didn't suffice (shh). I would get him to try submitting the physio claims online, but I was in the chair looking over his shoulder for when he had questions. I answered with "what do you think? If I weren't here, what would you do?" ... how fucking annoying of me, I know. But if I didn't get those neurons firing, he would adapt to always having and needing that help. I didn't want him to need that help, and I knew he didn't want to need it either. I knew if I didn't challenge him, he wouldn't achieve his goals and his recovery would plateau. This was me supporting his determination and drive to get better in the best way I saw fit.

I pushed him, and I was hard on him, but the intent was to help him. It was for his benefit, which I trusted he would realize later.

GRIEF

Grief is quite an emotion. I always used to think grief only occurred when someone passed away and you missed them. I felt strongly that without death, there was no grief.

Noa challenged me on this one day when I was describing my feelings towards my situation. I vividly remember her saying, "You know what you are feeling, right? You know what you are describing?"

I replied, "Sadness? Frustration?"

"No" she said, "this is grief."

Well, that makes no sense because last time I checked, both my parents were alive.

She then went on to explain to me that grief doesn't have to be the result of death. Grief is that heartache you get from missing something, losing something, or longing for a previous life you once had. My parents were still alive, but I had lost their good health. I had lost who my mom was before her addiction, and I had lost who my dad was before his accident. That was the one time I felt slightly resentful for having such amazing relationships with both of them.

I had experienced this form of loss and had finally come to realize that the emotion I feel so strongly every day *was grief.* It made me realize that grieving someone's death was not just the pain that their physical being was gone, it was the pain of losing that social, emotional, and intellectual connection you once had with them.

Someone can be standing right in front of you, but if they don't resemble the person you once knew, you can't help but feel they are gone.

Sometimes I question if that feeling of loss in a relationship with someone is worse than death itself.

I have also learned that grief is not linear. I like to think of it as a heart monitor, like the P-Q-R-S-T waves you see on the screen in the movies. Except grief is the slow-motion version of that. Sometimes it's up; things feel manageable, and you feel content. Sometimes it's in the middle; things could be worse but could be better. And sometimes it's quite low; things feel they are spiraling out of control and you're doggy paddling to keep your head above water.

What I've come to realize is that I can't change how or when grief hits. My organized self would prefer a set date and time when I will feel grief, with hourly reminders on my phone popping up until that point, so that I can properly prepare. Unfortunately, reality overrules my organized-freak self, and grief can hit at any moment without any warning, and you can't predict how severe that one will be.

Well, there's a challenge for my type-A personality if I ever saw one.

What I can do is ensure I have coping strategies at the ready, so that I am able to manage when it hits. I've had days where I feel good: no anxiety, no stress, no headaches, no chest pain. And then an hour later, I am in tears when a heavy wave of grief hits. It feels like a tsunami has hit my brain, but the longer I spend in counselling working through difficult emotions, the better I become at getting myself to the surface for air.

We need to create space for grief. In doing this, we healthily allow the process to occur without judgement of ourselves or others.

PARENTING MY PARENTS

Dad didn't feel that he needed counselling after his accident, but we all knew he did. This was part of the stigma of mental health. Dad grew up in a family where you don't talk about feelings or need help with anything. In fact, if you did, you looked *weak*. So naturally, trying to get him to see a counsellor before the brain injury would have been the same fight—and I can assure you he would never have gone, because he didn't need it, right? Walk it off!

His first comment when we asked him to go was, "well, I'm not crazy, so why would I do that?" This right here, in a nutshell, is what is wrong with how we speak about mental health—the stigma, the judgement that you must be certified psychotic to go see a counsellor. Well, that's just psychotic in itself, really. As Kat always says, "every person on this earth could benefit from a counsellor. Everyone."

Dad didn't talk about the trauma in his previous life. He has had a prosthetic eye since infancy, and this was a target for bullying in elementary school—luckily, he had older brothers who took care of those bullies pretty fast.

His parents died way too young, and if I grieve that loss without knowing them as an adult, I can't imagine what that grief was like for him.

He watched his brother die of alcoholism right in front of him, after his brother's wife tragically and suddenly passed away the year before. His brother just couldn't cope without his wife.

He experienced the loss of his brother-in-law, also named David. They were like true brothers, and David's life ended with a tragic overdose as well.

Dad would tell me how worried he was about Mom losing her life to alcohol. He was speaking from a place of real fear for his wife, but also a place of familiarity. Since he had seen a loved one pass from this same disease, he knew it was a very real possibility with Mom. Even though she was still in treatment, with occasional short visits home allowed, it was still a possibility.

Dad has had a lot of trauma and grief throughout his life, but never really addressed it.

Still, it was hard for him to deny that he needed help when he kept having major blowouts and wasn't able to explain why. Once, he got fired up at Mom because she didn't have her phone on her when Sunlife called. The anger wasn't warranted as there wasn't clear communication about this whatsoever. Another time, he forgot a couple things he needed from the grocery store, and his brain tricked him into thinking it was my fault. I started getting defensive, and he shot back. He started yelling *fuck you* at me over and over until I was screaming back and crying. Again, unwarranted anger that could have been avoided with simple communication.

Before his accident, he wouldn't have said "fuck you" to me if someone had a gun to his head telling him to. He would take the bullet before saying those words to me. This was the reality of the brain injury. I had to remember he still had outburst episodes, he was triggered easily, and he acted on impulse with little control over his behavior. Immediately after, he feels so bad that he hates himself. And I have to remind myself that we were warned about this threshold of anger; once it was reached, he wasn't able to control himself.

That part of his brain was gone. So, I guess it wasn't really his fault. It's moments like that I forgive but I will never forget. The scars will stay with me forever.

After that incident, he agreed to go to counselling. Once he admitted he didn't know why he did it, he knew he needed to at least figure that much out and see if there were ways to mitigate his anger. He agreed to one session, as a trial. How did we get him there? We said, "fine, if you don't see that you need it for yourself, that's okay, but then we *ask* that you do it for us. A gift to us." He has never been able to say no to a reasonable ask from his daughters.

I knew I still had a lot to unpack in counselling myself. One of my biggest anxiety-provoking issues was feeling the fear of the uncertainty in my parents' future. I felt terrible that they had both suffered such undeserving horrible circumstances. Having a recovering addict and a traumatic brain injured patient live together and try to coexist was an interesting combination. There was barely a full brain in the house put together, so you can imagine how quickly things turned sour when conflict or tension arose.

What was particularly sad was that my mother seemed unable to cope with my dad's injury. Plain and simple. I had a perfectly healthy brain—well, relatively speaking—and I still grieved parts of my dad's injury every day. This was not his fault; it's what was done to him, and I couldn't imagine how difficult it was for him every day. That being said, I admired him more than ever after watching him battle this recovery day in and day out. But that didn't mean I wasn't triggered with seeing deficits. That didn't mean it wasn't incredibly hard to witness.

I had flashbacks of the notebook entry she wrote on Oct 12th (Day 6):

OH DAVEY! Back on the sedation to protect your beautiful brain. Dr. Griesdale is so cautious with you. I do not like seeing you like this… not one bit. I desperately need for you to wake up.

My mom was not in a place in her recovery where she could cope with Dad's injury. She didn't see the smart, capable, independent, well-loved, athlete-man she married, and her brain would force her to sit in resentment and sadness about that rather than hope or acceptance. I thought maybe her recent relapses were simply due to her seeing this new life and being unable to live in it soberly. If she sat long enough in her past, she would drink. She could barely handle what her addiction had made her do, let alone manage this new world with a new version of her husband.

I saw the way she responded to him when he asked a question he had asked before. I saw the look on her face as she watched him struggle to do something he would have found easy before. I could read her thoughts as if they were written on her forehead; I could see this even when she was sober, but when she was drunk it was even more obvious.

Unfortunately, when she drank, the filter that helped her bite her tongue when she was sober was no longer present. When she was drunk, she would say what she was truly feeling: how he wasn't the same person anymore, how hard his injury was on her, that he wasn't her husband. That maybe he should have died.

You just can't take back those kinds of words. She could apologize all day long for saying those things while she was using, and we could forgive her while we blame the words on her disease. But no matter how many times she says she's sorry, her words still weigh heavy on him.

Many times, I heard them fighting from the office I was working in downstairs. I heard it and I cringed. I don't think it matters how old you are, hearing your parents fight is gut-wrenching, especially when they were both unpredictable in terms of their words and actions.

I would stop what I was doing and go sit at the bottom of the stairs, listening, seeing what the fight was about, trying to get a feeling for who started it or who was being more reasonable. Ultimately, I was just waiting to see if I needed to intervene to calm things down. I would sit there, biting my nails and scrolling through Instagram. They had never spoken like that to each other before in their lives. Hurtful words, powerful words, words that made me remember that neither of them were healthy. More often than not, a point would come at which I would have to intervene, usually because Dad was unknowingly coming off selfish with what he wanted done now and not later (a brain injury deficit) and this, understandably, frustrated Mom, or because Mom was getting so incredibly manipulative and purposely firing Dad up. She knew he had always had a temper, but now along with his brain injury, he was unpredictable. She pushed him until he exploded.

I actually witnessed her continue to do exactly what he'd asked her not to over and over and over. He asked her to walk away; she refused, and she continued the behavior she knew he hated. He tried to walk away, something I had taught him to do when she was not in her right mind like this, she followed him. If I got involved and she was rude to me, Dad got even more escalated. Then mom usually turned to me saying, "good job, Beth! Now Dad is even more angry at me! Is that what you wanted? Are you happy now? Great work!" The extreme sarcasm and insincerity in her voice pushed Dad over the edge. After multiple attempts for us both to stop her malicious verbal assaults, Dad was now so angry he was screaming in her face, threatening things I don't want to repeat.

I truly believe that at this point in her addiction, she needed another 'bad guy', for lack of a better term. She wanted to push us all to a breaking point so that we would say something—or do something—unforgivable, so that we would do things unrecognizable to our character. If we fell into this trap, she would have something to use against us, to show us that she's not acting like the only villain here. To show us that she's not the only one who has amends to make.

It was weird to feel like I was counselling them through their arguments, and it was becoming uncomfortably common. It was like two kids bickering about who said what or who did what; I heard, "well, he started it" or "then she said…" far too often for comfort. I was always able to de-escalate them, explaining Dad's perspective to Mom so that she would hear it better, and explaining Mom's to Dad so that he was reminded of the severity of her disease.

They needed that third party to translate their communication into more understandable language. I felt like I saw the future in these moments; it felt like I was coming between an argument of my two future kids. I was quickly snapped back into reality realizing these were my parents that I was parenting.

I felt proud when I was able to bring them to a point of apologizing to each other, seeing each other's perspectives, and feeling at ease again. But I was also warned by Noa that I should not be doing this. I was crossing a line that an adult child should never have to cross. This behavior could easily shift my relationship with both of them, in a negative way.

I should have been the child, and only the child. Not the counsellor, mentor, psychiatrist, or anyone else. I shouldn't have been suddenly muting myself and turning my video off in Zoom work meetings to run upstairs and settle things down. I shouldn't have had to think of excuses for why I missed work events just to cover up for the bullshit behind the scenes. But my fear got the best of me. I worried about the end result of some of these arguments if I didn't intervene. Two cognitively impacted individuals—I didn't want to see how that would end.

And I wondered why I hadn't moved out yet—it was fear.

At this point, I needed therapy more than I ever had before in my life. I needed to accept where both of my parents were in their recoveries while still maintaining my own boundaries. I needed to accept where my dad was in his recovery and continue being patient with the deficits. I was grateful that Mom was finally staying in treatment, but I still didn't want to talk to her. I was still hurt. I was still frustrated at her downplaying our experiences and denying the reality, even though I'm sure this was just a way to protect herself from more shame. She needed to feel the consequences of her behavior. Even though the addiction was out of her control, the actions to get help weren't. Just because you're in recovery trying to work a program, doesn't mean the past didn't happen. I was still stuck with working through that trauma, and every time I tried to work through it in the past, every time I just scraped the surface of understanding what the fuck happened in the last fifteen years, she would relapse. There was no time to process the past; there was only time to continue dealing with the present and to worry about the future.

When she had been in treatment for five months, it felt like I finally had the space and time to process that I never had before, which was a blessing and a curse. I had time to work through emotions, but the pain almost hit harder now because I had no distraction of a relapse to keep me from remembering Every. Single. Detail.

GUILT & WORRY, WORRY & GUILT

I was dealing with a lot of guilt. Guilt for leaving my grandma's house when she was lonely, to come home with Dad. Guilt for not doing the best that I could at work and being distracted with this chaos while trying desperately to be engaged with my clients. Guilt for the arguments and anger and things I said that I can't take back, for the times that walking away would have been the better path. I needed help navigating my feelings to learn what they meant and how to cope with them.

What's interesting about guilt is that it teaches us valuable lessons. Guilt is knowing you did something bad. But notice how the definition doesn't comment on you being bad as a person. Good people can do bad things and still be very good people.

The good thing about guilt is that it holds us accountable for who we want to be as humans, so feeling guilt just means you have a heart, and you know you want to choose differently next time. I believe even just feeling guilt in the slightest confirms you are a good person. We all make mistakes, but what separates good people from bad people is those that acknowledge their wrongdoings and make a conscious effort to avoid making those same mistakes again.

I still worry about what this stress and trauma has done—or is doing—to my brain and overall health. I know too well the effects of long-term chronically high cortisol levels. It *scares* me. So here I am doing therapy.

I worry about my future. I've always wanted kids. Four to be exact. I want to push to have a best-friend relationship with my kids like my mom had with us. This relationship she worked hard to build is everything I want to be as a mom. But I worry I'm too spent, too goddamn tired at age twenty-six. *What if* I don't regain the mental capacity and energy to create my own family. *What if* my child struggles with addiction. *What if* my child suffers a severe cognitive injury. I don't know if I can go through any of this again. *What if* I can't fully recover from this. *What if* I always have the brain fog. *What if* I never calm my anxiety. *What if* I can't forgive—forgive my mom, but also forgive myself. Forgive myself for putting my life on the back burner, for dropping career opportunities, for behaving in a way to others that reflects unresolved pain, for limiting my social bubble because I'm too drained to make time for everyone even though they all matter to me.

I worry about how my dad's injury will impact him as a future grandpa. Will a crying baby trigger him? Will he have the patience to manage a toddler? Will he be able to take them on adventures and hikes? Will he be able to teach them how to play soccer? Before his accident, these were no-brainers for him. He looked forward to this future and I knew he would be the best grandpa. What will this look like now?

I worry that this horrible relapse cycle will continue and that it won't just be me protecting myself, Kat, and Dad from this addiction, but my future kids as well. Before her addiction, I remember looking at my mom knowing she would be the world's best grandma. She was upbeat, funny, entertaining, and enthusiastic about kids. She was always in for an adventure and made the most out of any less-than-ideal situation. She would buy them fun toys, plan themed birthday parties for them, and always have treats in the house for when they came over. There was no doubt she would be a large part of their lives, and they would have been lucky to experience life with her. I now fear a life in which I am forced to put boundaries in place to keep those kids safe. I can see that future clearly if active addiction is still with us; they won't drive with her, they won't stay overnight with her, and they certainly won't be left alone with her. I fear this future of continued consequences and acts of desperation in an attempt to keep everyone safe. It *scares* me.

I worry about my relationship with my mom, and I constantly fear that I will always be in a place where I can't trust her. It's such a potentially real possibility at this time. I don't trust her, even when she's home and seemingly sober. It's usually a roller coaster, in and out of relapses, and that's when I find myself subconsciously doing things that make it clear that I don't trust her.

When Dad needs a ride to ICBC on a day that I work, she agrees to take him. But I cannot help but wonder if I will have to cancel on that client minutes before because she's drinking.

I give her tasks in Dad's recovery to try to share the load, but my brain convinces me I'll just be doing it myself after she bails on it anyways.

When we went to Kat's graduation for her nurse practitioner masters, I assumed Mom wouldn't show up; why wouldn't I, given the last graduation situation.

I can't let her take Dad to town for his GF Strong driving rehab assessment because there's such a good chance of her drinking the night before and not being able to start the car (there is currently a breathalyzer in the car) or drinking while he's there so they are stuck and can't get home. He doesn't need that added stress on top of test day, so I take a vacation day from work so that I'm the one who can take him. I know this way he will get there and home safely.

I want her to go to his next psychiatry appointment with him so that she can help him articulate his needs, but due to my lack of trust, I also booked that day off in case I'm needed.

I still can't have her driving my car; I don't trust it won't end up in a ditch or, at the very least, with cigarette smoke staining the inside. I still don't get into a car with her driving either, even when she is sober. I have flashbacks of her driving recklessly and half asleep, blowing through stop signs or changing lanes on a whim without shoulder checking. I tried getting into a car with her last year for the first time in a long time. She drove safe, but I still couldn't help but be anxious the entire time. I wanted out. I don't know that I'll ever be able to drive with her again from this trauma.

And yes, some of these things never happened; she never ended up bailing on the ICBC drive. She did show up for Kat's grad. She did go to Dad's psychiatry appointment. But there's always a good chance she will not follow through. She has fallen short due to her addiction so many times, there's no predicting whether the next ask will happen or not, her prior agreement to it was no guarantee. At the end of the day, I have no trust for her at all, for now. Hopefully that will change over time, but it will only change with changed behavior.

I worry about finances. I watched my parents go from having the world by its tail to really having to watch what comes in and out of the bank. I saw my dad struggle trying to ensure he could save enough money on the side to keep for her treatment. He had big ideas, big plans that he wanted to invest his money into, mostly revolving around the future for myself and Kat. A lot of those ideas got thrown out the window with the shear cost of treatment. As a result, I've started saving money with more intention. I keep an account in my bank that is stored in case Mom goes through another severe relapse and needs long term inpatient treatment again. I don't want the bulk of that to fall on my dad and his future. I want to step up to help next time and I intend to with this saved money. But I worry about how long I must save it before using it for my own future.

I worry every time I hear a helicopter. Not only does it remind me of when dad needed one, but it makes my heart sink thinking of the family that is holding their breath at that moment for the person inside.

I never would have predicted how mentally exhausting this can be. I guess I never had that type of mental stress back in high school; again, what privilege. I compare it to athletics. I had been dead out of breath many times, but not a lot of my exhaustion had hit me as hard as this had:

Soccer sprints? *Didn't compare.*

Volleyball? Diving, jumping, back-to-back games... *Nah.*

Half marathons? *Not the same.*

Triathlons? *Meh.*

Doing 2k sprints on an erg with our UBC Varsity Rowing team? *Fuck that was fucking tiring, and I can vividly remember laying on the ground hearing my heart beat through my ears. I could feel the lactic acid building up in my legs. I can still taste the blood from breathing so hard in and out. It just felt like I couldn't get enough air in no matter how much I tried. They call it the paper bag 2k – hyperventilate first, vomit after. Horribly exhausting, but this was still not comparable.*

That's what is so eye-opening – I thought I knew *exhaustion.* I thought I had seen it many times. But what's the difference here? These sports... well, first of all they're exhilarating, so that's an added benefit, but they also result in *physical* exhaustion. Your legs shake, you can't lift your arms the next day, walking up and down stairs feels like you're seventy years older than you are. But you go into a hot tub, rub some Voltaren on there, and the aches reside after a number of days. This is not the same as *mental* exhaustion, where you can't just fix it with some anti-inflammatory cream and a warm bath. I never thought I could be *more* tired from chasing an addict or managing a brain injured patient, than I was with athletics. But they really didn't compare. When I was dealing with mom in an addict episode, it *felt like* I'd run a marathon, except the pain didn't come from my legs, it came from my head and my heart.

People always joked around saying "you're always yawning, how do you go to bed at eight PM, why are you always so tired!" And I would always just laugh and shrug, but I remember thinking to myself "if only you knew." I never used to be like this. I used to be full of energy all the time. But this mental exhaustion hit me so damn hard, I felt drained constantly.

I have also significantly reduced my drinking. I never drank heavy, and it was never an issue, but I definitely had some rowdy nights back in high school and University. Alcohol has left my family with deep wounds, and it has impacted my life more negatively than I could have ever imagined. Although I don't think I have the genetic predisposition to addiction, I feel like I can't be careful enough, because I know if you asked my mother at my age, she would never have predicted this future for herself and her family. I think alcohol itself gives me some form of PTSD, so I steer clear for now. Maybe one day when I'm more healed, I will feel less anxious having a drink or two.

Noa still remains amazing in my counselling sessions. She has reassured me that I've done everything I can for my mother, more than any other client and client's family she has ever had. She praises me on my hard work and effort in my dad's recovery. She reminds me to take care of myself when I forget. She teaches me coping strategies. She teaches me how to manage resentment. She teaches me what to do in a panic attack, how to calm my central nervous system.

She explains again the irrational behavior of anxiety, how it thrives off illogical thoughts, how its best friend is lack of control. She explains to me why I get nervous now for things I never used to be nervous for, like Zoom meetings or friend hangouts—my central nervous system has basically been hijacked, and unfortunately my body has adapted to expecting a threat. Things in my life that never should have been a threat, became one, so my body has a hard time differentiating what is safe and what isn't, so it assumes all is not. I can feel my blood pressure rise and heart rate increase, as a result of preparing for that irrational threat.

I need therapy more than ever. I need to heal what has been so viciously damaged. I want my old self back.

NIGHTMARES

Mom had remained in treatment since she begrudgingly agreed to go back when Dad threatened divorce back in late August of 2020. In early 2021, she was, to my surprise, still there, at Westminster House Women's Inpatient Treatment Centre. This was the six-month mark, the longest time she had ever spent in a treatment facility.

I remember feeling shocked, like it wasn't real or that she had escaped unknowingly and had actually been somewhere else that whole time. She always used to find a short cut with treatment: leaving MIA or before she was recommended to be discharged. I was proud of her that she spent this long getting the help she needed, but I still wasn't ready to invest in a relationship with her. I wasn't opposed at that time to keeping that door open for the future, but she had a lot of work to do. She needed to work on unwarranted resentment towards family members, seeing things from other peoples' perspectives, and showing some vulnerability and humility.

I have high standards and expectations from her now, but I knew I needed to do this years ago. I've had to put boundaries in place, and until I am ready and strong enough to try again at the relationship, she just has to be patient and wait. Those boundaries are my safety net. I have a lot to process and work through. I was worried that this would be difficult, holding the boundary while I was Dad's main caregiver at home, but it was actually easier given she was in treatment. This physical distance helped me start to heal from the past.

I have my own resentments I need to work through. I need to work through them because at the end of the day, they were due to her extreme sickness, regardless of how much they pained me. I resent her for the anxiety that has trickled into every area of my life—to my career, my friends, my family, and my social skills, which have all taken a hit from it. I think everyone around me is judging me even though I'm sure nobody is. I feel urgency to do things all the time to keep my body and mind busy. I wonder if I'm not enough and what I could be doing more of. I would even get worried about going out on dates; I used to be fearless but that changed to me thinking, *what if the guy kills me? What if he locks me up and rapes me? What if I get tortured?* Anxiety is irrational, like I said, but it feels so incredibly real.

I get frustrated that this isn't a quick fix, that I need to invest time and energy into gaining back what I naturally had. I resent her for the family relationships we have lost; those losses can all be traced back to her addiction behaviours. I resent her for having Dad's caretaking fall on me—not just for the demands of the job itself, but for what it's done to our relationship, from best friends to a role reversal. It's a difficult space to be in. I resent just simply not having a mother for the past fifteen years; the missed opportunities are countless. But I need to remember this wasn't her choosing. She would never choose to make me feel this way. She would never choose to do this. This disease is just so powerful. So damn powerful.

Dad was doing well, although there was the question of whether he had plateaued in recovery. We weren't entirely sure; there were days when he seemed to be improving and days where he seemed stalled. We knew we would simply take as much as we could get. His motivation continued to be inspiring. We weren't sure work was possible, but he was determined to go back. He worked on his physiotherapy religiously. He always had big goals, and I never had a doubt he would achieve them.

Mom was getting ready to come home. She had been in treatment now for eight months. I still believed that she needed at least one year in treatment before the move home, and the professionals in the treatment centre agreed. I had a hard time understanding why she was unwilling to stay for four more months. *Isn't a full year in treatment worth it if it could potentially mean gaining back the next thirty years of your life?* However, Mom was never intending to stay longer than thirty days, and she was itching to get out.

There was of course the concern that she wouldn't maintain sobriety at home, given her track record. But the bigger concern wasn't when she was coming home, but what she was coming home to. We all knew it was a different life with Dad in his own rehab, and myself with the boundaries I had maintained with her. It felt more like sober time was accomplished, but I questioned whether the work was put in to learn how to cope with these difficult situations at home. There wasn't anything we could do about the discharge, we had to just accept that she felt confident in her recovery, feel grateful that she stayed for the time that she did and be hopeful that it would result in a successful continued recovery at home.

Westminster House set her up with some short-term transitions home, just to see how things went. She would come home for a weekend, and head back to treatment to assess how things went with her team there. She would then come home for three to four days, and head back to assess what went well and what could have been improved.

This quickly led to the full transition home. The dynamics at home were uncomfortable, especially as I tried to maintain a strong boundary with her. Dad was remaining hopeful that she would never relapse again; this was one of the deficits of his injury. He didn't remember how severe her past was. I, on the other hand, was constantly skeptical of her sobriety, not trusting even one day of it and just waiting for the relapse to come. I knew she had some good skills from treatment to stay on track, but I also knew she had zero skills to cope with a brain-injured husband on a daily basis. She was fairly diligent with her morning and evening meetings, staying in touch with her sponsor, trying to get a sponsee for herself so she could practice the leadership role too, and working on her steps. I was starting to ease off a bit and gain some trust as a couple months went by; she seemed to be hanging on to her sobriety.

She relapsed, just a few days before her one-year cake in August 2021. She was so, so close to a massive milestone. She blamed it on us, of course. She claimed she didn't feel we were going to celebrate it with her, so she decided *fuck it* and drank. They really will use any excuse in the book; why the hell would we not celebrate one year of sobriety with her? Regardless of the past, we have always risen above and celebrated the *good* in her recovery. Always. It was actually kind of a slap in the face that she even thought we wouldn't and used that as her reason that she caved. I knew deep down that this was not the reason she relapsed. I knew she relapsed because of some need that was unmet, some fear that was only felt by her, or some pain that was unresolved.

She did try to deny her lack of sobriety, but I knew this game all too well. It was the little things I was far too familiar with: the way her smile curved funny instead of normal, the way her eyes had a glossy filter over them, the way her eyes squinted with her eyelids moving a bit too slow, the way her tone of voice sounded unaware and confused, the slight delay in response to questions, the way she sat with her left shoulder slightly lower than her right, the way she walked, the way she looked around the room, the way she rubbed her hands together, how her hair was done, the texture of her skin. No one would notice these things, but I knew the red flags like the back of my hand. Dad used to say the same thing, that you could walk through the door and take one look at her and just know. I was starting to be able to identify the relapse patterns from a distance too: the lack of communication, not texting back, or texting back in a way she wouldn't normally text. These signs always meant a relapse. These signs never lied.

I had been out golfing with my friends that day, but I remember leaving the pitch & putt shortly after my first shot to head home as the relapse escalated. I sucked at golf anyways, and I had to make sure mom was controlled and dad was protected.

I felt bad that she got that close to a massive milestone and then relapsed. I felt really, really bad for her. But it's always fifty-fifty, isn't it? I also felt so frustrated that we were back here again. I felt angry that we were back in a place we could have predicted. I felt annoyed that this horrible outburst could have been avoided with a few words of honesty. And as I said, I'm not as compassionate in that moment, not when I've had to put my life aside once again because hers got so out of hand. I gave her a chance to be honest before I left to go golfing, and she wasn't. That would have been the moment that changed the outcome. That was the moment I was compassionate. Honesty will always be met with compassion. But I guess that's just the addict brain. The lying and manipulative behavior all comes with the addiction itself. You can't have one without the other.

Noa had been reminding me to continue my coping strategies. She challenged me to sit with feelings rather than race for distraction. For a long time, I had been running away from thoughts and feelings, and replacing them with actionable items. One example was attending my work meetings on my days off. I loved my dietitian team, so I enjoyed the meetings, but this was also a sign of how desperate I was to be in a different space mentally on a Wednesday and Friday morning. No matter the stress I faced in my workday, it was a break from this reality. It was good to have distractions, but I needed to learn to cope at some point too. I needed to stop running. I knew I couldn't outrun my problems, and even when I tried, they seemed to consistently have better endurance than me.

Most recently, I have been struggling to manage the nightmares.

I have nightmares of Mom overdosing in a room that I can't get into and I'm panicking trying to break down the door and my phone died so I can't call 911 and I'm sweating and crying and screaming.

I have nightmares of walking into the room and seeing her body frozen, and as I walk towards her, I realize it's stuck in rigor mortis. I see her pale face. I put my hand out and can feel her skin, ice cold. The shock of the cold skin has shaken me awake.

I have nightmares of having mom removed from the house, changing the locks, and telling her it's either this homeless life or treatment – you choose. In this nightmare, she leaves the house and I later find her dead in a homeless shelter. I can see where she slept on the floor. I can see the familiarity of the one shirt and pair of pants she has with her. I can feel the darkness in the room. I wake up shaking with those images, knowing very well how real they could be one day. I'm left feeling the intense weight of the risk that type of ultimatum holds.

I have nightmares of walking up my street and seeing something in the ditch ahead of me. As I walk towards it, I cringe as I notice the orange mountain bike and realize the thing in the ditch is my dad. It's the scene described to me detailing where his accident started. I run up to him screaming while desperately reaching for my phone to call 911. The entire injury starts from square one in this nightmare.

I have nightmares of Dad's first day in the ER—I see the trauma bay doors sliding open and closed repeatedly while I'm desperately scanning for him. I'm haunted by the look of him on life support, this image I can't get out of my head.

I have nightmares of Dad's days of severe memory loss, but in these nightmares, he doesn't end up remembering us and I kick myself awake at this thought.

I have nightmares that my dad gets into a fight with someone, and I have to run to this person fast enough to warn him that if you hit him, you'll kill him. I have to scream at them to stop because they aren't aware of his injury.

I have nightmares that my mom uses, is out of her mind, can't manage her grief with Dad's new state, and ends his life herself. I have woken up screaming from this one, drenched in a pool of my own sweat.

Sometimes I wake up in the middle of night from these nightmares. Other times I just get a large twitch in my body as I'm dozing off to sleep; I wake suddenly from the twitch, and I quickly realize it wasn't real.

Sometimes it's not even a nightmare, it's just lying awake for hours having suddenly lost the ability to shut my mind off. I start thinking of things that upset me and I can't shake them off. I can't stop the images from playing. I can't quiet my brain. I find myself in tears and I can't stop crying. I'm trying to be quiet because I don't want to wake anyone, especially my partner, Brydon, as I'm lying right beside him. I always forget how silent the house is at two in the morning.

Sometimes it passes after an hour or so, sometimes it's many hours. Noa tells me I should get out of bed and walk around when this happens. Although shoving my covers over and exposing my body to the cold air is literally the last thing on earth I want to do, she has yet to fail me on guidance and sure enough, it does seem to work. I'm not looking forward to admitting that to her next week.

I have no warning when these nights are coming, and I can't even pinpoint what exactly I'm in tears over. It just hits, and when it hits, I can't seem to stop it. It's just my body telling me I need to get this out, this is the safest time and place to do so, so just let me do this. And eventually I exhaust myself into falling asleep.

Noa has explained to me what this is and why it happens. Apparently, I'm good at tricking myself into thinking I'm recovered, that I'm okay. The nightmares are an undeniable reminder that I'm not. When we lie in bed trying to fall asleep, anxiety sees this as an opportunity to thrive (that's annoying as fuck). Finally, it's quiet. I can't distract myself with day-to-day routines at this hour because it's time for quiet and sleep. This is when you truly know where your mental health stands. And this is when I realized I'm not actually coping at all, I'm just distracting myself until my mind is undistracted.

Part of coping and taking care of myself is having a different approach to Mom's addiction now. We have run around exhausting ourselves in the past trying to get her to detox, then treatment, then to stay in treatment. But at the end of the day, what we've been shown time after time is that she is the only one that can make these decisions.

I struggle with this because I wonder if she's just unable to make good decisions because of her damaged brain, but we've been told by the experts again and again that we have no control here. All we can do is offer to take her to treatment, remind her it's worth the money, and support her by continuing to give her advice when she asks. But we can't force her. We have tried this way for years and years, and all it results in is her building resentments towards us and us feeling like we have failed yet again. Nobody wins.

I have a hard time taking care of myself, as I'm sure many of my readers do as well. It sounds like a good thing, a productive thing, a selfless thing. But in reality, it's just plain stupid. It took me until the age of twenty-seven to learn how to take care of myself, and I still struggle with it. I feel like I'm not enough when I'm not doing fourteen things at once. I go to sit down and I feel immediate guilt thinking about the things I could be doing with that time. I have to repeat to myself in my head over and over again the reasons why it's okay to be taking this time to slow down.

I did my workout with my friend Maddy this morning, I did some online course work, I took Dad to the doctor, and later I have an appointment with his neurologist and a walk with my friend Renee. So, it's okay to take this minute to chill out. You earned it.

I'm going to Brydon's tonight. But should I? Did I do enough today to deserve that "time off?"

Okay, I'll watch TikTok for fifteen minutes only IF I remain productive the next twenty minutes.

I want to sleep in this morning, but I will miss my workout. I guess I can skip it, but only IF I make up for it later today with a workout or do a longer workout tomorrow.

An outing with friends this weekend, going away? I'll have to work extra hard this week to make sure I feel I'm "allowed" to go, that I'm "deserving" of it.

This is not me boasting. This is me being honest about a true character flaw. I love being productive, I've always been like that. But if you take it too far, as I tend to do, it's a form of self-punishment. It's not healthy to feel we need reasons to do things that make us relaxed or happy. I grew up learning to thrive in that busy, somewhat chaotic environment. I believe a lot of that came from both my parents; my dad always being productive, and my mom always thriving in that busy, 'doing-one-million-things-at-once' state. But in our day and age, constant stress and resisting rest can actually lead to some serious mental, physical and emotional consequences. I beat myself to burnout trying to keep myself accountable to the unrealistic standard I had set.

I look back now and realize so many of my actions were the result of this feeling. I went hard with sports—being on the teams wasn't enough, I wanted to be captain and lead the team. Being in first year university and only doing academics wasn't enough, so I took up half marathon running, destroying my knees along the way. I always strived to be on a varsity team, so rowing for UBC was next.

I needed something after rowing ended so triathlons came into the picture. Between triathlon trainings, it would be regular workouts every day of the week. I pushed until I achieved these goals. This may have been simply my drive for distraction, or it was my drive for adrenaline; there's no rush like crossing the finish line after hours of physical exhaustion or firing the soccer ball into the back of the net when the game is tied and there's only minutes remaining. But even if it was seeking adrenaline, that was arguably a distraction in itself.

Academics took a similar toll; I love school, I love learning, I love being a student. I want to do well. So, I went to school for seven years and I'm still on and off doing online courses to further my education.

I was thrown into caretaking at a young age; I could have done the bare minimum for my mom and dad, but I wouldn't let myself off the hook for that. It had gotten to the point where I felt I had let them become dependent on me, and I would feel guilty whenever I left the house.

I didn't utilize my sick days at work. I would work from home with a cold, or flu, or covid. It wasn't until I had viral laryngitis that I needed to take a sick day (a little hard to counsel clients without a voice), but even then, I remember feeling guilty. If it wasn't guilt, then it was a feeling of staying competitive with myself in keeping my 'no-sick-days' streak alive. *What the fuck is wrong with me?*

I always feel I'm not doing enough if I'm not doing the next best thing.

I started visiting one of my best friends ninety-year-old grandpa; he's blind but has a heart of gold and we both enjoy our weekly chats.

I'm driven to start my own business; this had become my next obsession.

And now I'm continuing to write this book.

I take these things on because they make me feel good. They make me feel worthy. They make me feel *enough*. But it's a slippery slope, only allowing yourself to feel deserving of anything if you meet a specific rule you have in place. It's a slippery slope as I wonder if that in itself is a form of addiction… addiction to constantly competing, when the only competition is myself.

It took me a long time to realize why I live like this. Yes, some of it is just simply in my genes, a learned behavior. And yes, as above, it makes me feel good, worthy, and enough. But with enough therapy, I've also realized it's partly from the things that have happened to me. I feel a need to prove I'm better than the things that have happened to me. I'm better than my past. I guess I need and crave the distraction—studying, training, writing—it's all a distraction from what's going on behind the scenes. But it's also about the control – feeling a desperate need to control the things I can in my life to make up for the severe lack of control addiction has shown me.

As Noa likes to put it, "Hyper-independence is a trauma response."

That quote resonated with me so hard that I actually felt less of a need to do those things after hearing it.

She explained to me how trauma is what's behind a lot of these actions. She reminds me to "name it" first: name the feeling, name the obsession, name your thoughts. She also reminds me that mindfulness and meditation are great for trying to get out of the mental cycle.

I still struggle with this. And again, it's not a good thing. It's something I need to work hard on to let myself slow down. Let myself enjoy life and stop taking it so seriously. I need to let myself be taken care of, and be supported, whatever that may look like.

And let's be clear—taking care of yourself looks different for everyone, so whatever it takes, just know what works for you. For me, it's writing things down, meditating, working out, and humor. And I know that's dark, but if I can make light of things or laugh about things, it does help me cope with them.

Above all, I hope learning to cope helps manage the nightmares.

EMOTIONAL TORTURE: PART 1

I was hoping 2022 would be a different year for Mom, an opportunity to turn things around and have a fresh start.

I don't know why I got hopeful for these things anymore.

I'll never forget watching her lie around, staring at the walls, earbuds in, tuned out of the world. It went on for days, weeks, months. Not only was it triggering to watch from every past behavior that resembles relapse, but it was incredibly sad. It was another mixture of pure anger and genuine compassion. I didn't know if it was drinking, new drug experimentation, or severe depression. It seemed selective, making it hard to draw any solid conclusions.

I felt angry at what looked like a lack of motivation for life on her part; after everything we've been through, I still had to come home to this state, this trance, this lifeless person. Then I would feel the wave of compassion—if this was true depression, she didn't have the chemicals in her brain to do anything more. This isn't her fault. But really, I think I only got angry because I wanted so badly for it to be different. I wanted a future for my dad, and I wanted to repair my relationship with my mom. So, what was the solution then? I couldn't force her to go see her practitioner, start taking the appropriate medication, and care about her health like I did. But I also could barely stand to see her in this state any longer.

So, Dad and I agreed to try the hands-off approach. We tried to ignore these states when we saw them, letting it ride out until the good day(s) came. But this approach was way easier said than done and the good days were becoming more and more infrequent.

Nothing I said could make her realize the severity of the situation. I could verbally paint her pictures of the traumas she put us through the night before. I could remind her she won't have anything to do with my future kids if she doesn't take action to get help. I could threaten my own relationship with her. I guess she started feeling numb to that one. I even told her I couldn't stand who she was, and I desperately wanted it over, whether that meant she lived or died.

Of course, half of me didn't even know if I believed I felt that way. Half of me felt, and still feels, sick to my stomach for saying it out loud to her. But the other half of me was barely hanging on by a thread to this life with her, this life that was putting all of us, including her, in severe pain.

Nothing was enough for her to see the reality. No words could make her go to treatment, and even if they could, she would be going to shut us up, to come home to say, "there, I did thirty days, now back off." I knew if she wasn't going for the right reasons—because she saw the NEED to go—she would never be successful. That's a prime example of the nocebo response actually, the type of response where someone believes something won't work, which ultimately results in it not working. She literally convinces herself it won't help, so she doesn't go through all the steps and all the work, and it inevitably, and unsurprisingly, doesn't get her any better. But of course, there's much more than a nocebo response here, there's the power of the drug – nothing would entice her more than it would, and nothing could make her get help if it resulted in the pure fear of going somewhere without that drug, that pain numbing drug.

She's always turned mean when she drinks, but somehow, she's gotten meaner. She slips into the victim cries for help. She drunk cries and verbally abuses those around her.

"I just want the old Dave back" she says to my dad, again and again.

When he gets frustrated, she says, "it's okay, I'll end it all soon." Ah, the suicide threat again. It always comes back to bite us in the ass. It's so incredibly unfair to verbally abuse him then make him feel like he'll be the reason you kill yourself if you jump off a bridge tomorrow. It's cognitively draining for anyone, let alone a brain-injured patient, where the trauma continues to the injured organ.

And again, I still didn't truly believe she was actually going to take action to kill herself. One time I called her out and told her I thought she was bluffing all for the purpose of changing our course of action. She asked why I thought she was bluffing, and I told her that she had opportunity to kill herself and didn't take it. I pointed out the rope in the back yard hanging off the trees, the cliff at the end of the trail that hooks to our backyard, the knives in the kitchen drawer… I reminded her that I knew she didn't want to die, because if she did, she would have already done it. I felt like this was a bit of a dark conversation, obviously I wasn't intending to make her aware of her 'ways out' but I was simply pointing out that her threats were simply just that: threats. But then of course I hear the voice in my head that does force me to back off: *maybe this time she is serious. Don't push her and have her prove you wrong here; this isn't something you want to be wrong about.* So, I shut up.

She has started talking about doing the MAID program. This was unsettling to hear for all of us, but especially for grandma as we had recently gone through this program for Whooee's passing. It was hard to hear her planning for her own death and it was difficult to tell if she was serious or if this was just another attention grab.

I did investigate something called a "react case" that was newly available on the coast. I didn't know a lot about it, but it sounded like a useful tool for us to have in our toolbox. The tricky part was that several events needed to occur in order for it to be successful, and these things seemed unlikely in our given circumstances.

First of all, Dad would have had to admit he felt his safety was at risk living with her. He had yet to admit this, and I didn't think he would, because he's never wanted to show us those emotions in this addiction. Even if he did say these words to us, he would have had to repeat them again to the mental health team, which didn't happen and was unlikely to ever happen.

Then, Mom and Dad would each be interviewed separately. A decision would be made that would include Mom being allowed to live at home, but under very strict boundaries—I never figured out exactly what these boundaries looked like, but I believe it was some form of check-ins and accountability measures. Then, if Mom did not abide by these rules, there was the potential for having her removed from the house. I didn't know where, but I didn't need to at that moment. I just needed the reassurance that there was this option around if Dad did start to feel unsafe. I had explained to him how it worked, and who to call if he wanted to re-visit this option. I had of course reminded him he can always call 911 if things got out of hand and I wasn't around. His safety was a big priority at this time.

It was less than twenty-four hours after having this conversation that I was calling the cops myself. Things had gotten progressively worse. Mom was drinking most days, and when she is drunk, she is both verbally and physically abusive. The verbal is more common, the harsh words, the *fuck offs*, the repeated disclosure that she doesn't have her true husband.

She had started hitting when she drank—sometimes it was a little fling of her hand, sometimes it was a couple of punches to the arm. She seemed to be in a psychotic state when she did this.

So, I made the decision, like I have many times in the past, to call the cops. I make these decisions carefully to ensure I'm not in the wrong, but I figured this was probably something I should have done three months prior. It was overdue this time. I figured she couldn't choose to both refuse treatment AND live in a family home like this. I called the non-emergency number and asked them to call my mom's phone to do a mental health check-in. Once they understood the circumstances, they easily complied. They agreed to call her and not drop by the house because I warned them this may give my dad a lot of anxiety. So I thought, *okay, good, they will call her and warn her this is serious. They will explain the potential consequences of her behavior if she is refusing help. I can get back to my day now.*

I had an important meeting that morning that I had planned for months. It was an online meet-up with a pelvic floor physio to discuss how gut health and the pelvic floor are interrelated. This lady was hard to track down since she is an expert in her field, so it was something I really didn't want to miss. It was live to both my online audience, and hers too. I started the meeting on time as I tried to forget about the conversations from that morning.

It wasn't until Mom barged into my office and said, "the cops are here, and they want to talk to you" that I started getting shaky and distracted. I continued to nod my head to the physio without even turning from my screen towards my mother, continued to act as though I was listening, but my mind was elsewhere from that moment on.

I tried to breeze past it hoping nobody in the audience heard my mom blurt out that the cops were in my driveway. I think I would hesitate before working with a dietitian who's being pulled out of a meeting to go talk to the police. I accepted at that moment I wouldn't be getting any future clients from this chat.

Next the cop came into the office, saw I was on a virtual call, and slowly backed out. Clearly I was needed in the conversation going on outside. *Fuck.*

I tried so hard to focus in the last bit of this live discussion, but my brain was just blank, and I wasn't hearing a word the physio was saying. I ended up having to wrap it up earlier than I wanted to, thanking her for coming and hoping she didn't notice my abrupt ending to the conversation.

I went outside to see what was going on.

It's nice and sunny out. Too bad I'm dealing with this shit show again instead of sitting here working on my tan. I love when my freckles come out from the sun. But the frecks will have to wait, because the cop is staring at me.

The cop was standing there waiting for me to chat with her. She pulled me aside and explained that she came in person because no one answered the phones. She called Mom, no answer, of course. She called me twice, but I was in the meeting and was forced to ignore it. I remembered doing this to a couple of no-caller-IDs during my meeting, which I now understand was the cops trying to call me. They have no choice but to come to the house when this occurs because they don't know what that means in terms of safety; obviously it's a huge red flag when no one answers the phone.

I talked to her for a while, explained the situation. She was quite sympathetic and assured me I had done the right thing. She repeated numerous times that I must call 911 as soon as any physical or suicidal ideations start again, whether it's in the day or the middle of the night. She then spoke to my mom and dad separately.

I felt so bad for my dad. And of course, I felt bad for my mom, but it felt like my dad was a domestic violence victim, his fears still outweighing his actions. He was so fearful with Mom's constant suicide threats that he didn't make big moves to push her. He hadn't called 911 himself during this time because he was terrified it would force her to flee and then kill herself, and he would have to live with that forever. I get that. I get that completely. But he was also convinced she was getting better, because she took advantage of his poor memory and was able to make him believe she wasn't drunk the past seven days; her last drunken episode was three weeks prior, if not more!

No. It was the day before, actually, and it had been going on for weeks and months—years if you want to get literal. He believes it's her last time using every single time, first because she is extremely believable, second because his memory isn't super clear on her past, and third because I do believe some part of her brain really wants sobriety and convinces her it's doable, despite not taking the proper steps to recovery.

But I'm not this gullible anymore, I've seen it for far too long to believe that bullshit. I wish my dad had that part of his old brain to remind himself this wasn't over as long as she lived at home and continued recovery in the half-assed way that she did. She relapses and he's so upset. This is when he wants to take action to call the cops and get her to detox. Then she spends eight hours sober, and he's convinced she's better and that was her last relapse. This is when he doesn't want to take the harsh approach anymore if "she's better." Then she relapses again and he's back to being upset. This cycle continues. I don't think it's him not remembering the relapse, it's just him putting all his emotion into hope, regardless of all the past pattern pointing towards this never being successful from home.

I still fear she will die in that house if we don't keep forcing help upon her. But that's just it, isn't it? We either force her to go to treatment and she kills herself on the way there, or we don't force her anywhere and watch her slowly die here. We lose either way. There is no winning.

I think this cops' arrival really shook my mom. As I said, it's not foreign whatsoever to call the cops, but it had been a year or so since we last called them, which was an extremely long time given our history. I think she was getting confident - confident she had convinced my dad she was getting better despite the obvious, confident she could trick us, and confident she could have both a drunk and sober life whenever she chose. Not on my watch. If you want to play hard ball, sign me up and I'll play too.

Not even a week later and she was back to crying at night, telling Dad how sad she was about our relationship. The issue? It was drunk crying. It's the triangle game of manipulating Dad to have him feel bad for her, and in turn, have him tell me that she's really trying, and she wants our relationship to be better. Of course, I will always keep that door open for her, but it had only been six days since the last relapse and enduring the abuse that came along with it. Repairing relationships takes time, I can't stress that enough. She expects to have the past forgotten with a few days of sobriety under her belt that I know aren't going to last. Even though I know her past actions weren't within her conscious control, I still need time before re-investing in a relationship before it's ready to evolve properly. Dad knows better at this time than to have her convince him I'm unfair towards her. They are called boundaries, they are to protect myself and our relationship, and I already felt that I may have been late to the game implementing them.

This was the evening that she not only manipulated the situation to make me look bad again, but she told Dad she was going to kill herself and leave a note in her PJs that said, "you're welcome, Beth."

I can't even put into words how that feels. The sadness, hurt, shock—not really since it's not the first time—but also the frustration, resentment, disbelief, and anger. I decided I just couldn't be in the house that night. So, I grabbed a pillow, two blankets, and my phone and took them to my car. I drove up the street and slept there in my car. The silence was relieving.

In the addict brain, while mustering up the ways to explain the inappropriate behaviour, it's all about who to toss the blame onto. It's about how you can manipulate a situation to make sure you're not the only one who looks "bad." As long as someone else looks shitty too, you're perceived as less of a problem in the eyes of those around you, right?

I had been in contact with her sponsor. More times than not, I had reached out to her for advice or guidance, but a couple times she initiated the conversation to ask about how Mom was doing.

It was a tricky situation— I was honest with her sponsor, but it seemed this created a lot of tension once it was in the open how much mom had been lying to her. She would say things are great, she was fine, no problems, when really the cops were there the day before, she had been aggressively drunk at least once a week, and her daughters were continuing to remove her from their lives to get away from the chaos. *So, not super fine then???*

So, Mom's sponsor had to be transparent with her. She had to tell Mom that she had heard from me and knew exactly what was going on in the house. What did this create? A situation in which mom was furious with me, telling me that if her sponsor left her, it was on me. We all knew that if her sponsor left her, it was on *her*. She was the one creating a dishonest relationship, but she had conveniently used my communication with her sponsor as a perfect target for blame if things went south. Now if her sponsor actually left her, it was my fault, because if I hadn't told her sponsor how things were really going, she would never have lost her in the first place. She had me to blame.

We even tried counselling together. I wasn't entirely ready for this, but I figured if she wanted to work at our relationship, I shouldn't shut that down. We tried a couple times, but it was unsuccessful.

The first time there was lying and denial in the sessions, which made it impossible to move forward. The second time she was busy using, didn't attend, and I had the familiar feeling of her not showing up for me. The third time, the counsellor actually suggested we commit to three months of no contact, and she didn't think she was a good fit for us. Guess we scared that one off.

More lying. Just straight to our faces lying. She would say she's in a meeting, but I could see her screen in the reflection of the window behind her. Unless NA meetings have become an optional dress-up-as-a-clown night, I'd say she's on Netflix watching a show with clowns in it.

If it wasn't lying, then it was a threat. Usually the classic threat of suicide, or sometimes something less severe. The threats got us where she wanted us. They made us back off with our actions, take back our words, and stay quiet.

For example, Kat had recently cut her out and created a boundary in which she would only communicate with her if mom went to treatment. I had done the same. We were that desperate. Mom was so angry about this that she threatened to end her life. This felt unfair considering we were only taking these measures to try to push her into getting help. If she didn't threaten to kill herself, she would do something else that divided us, like telling the family she is not attending Easter dinner in two weeks, knowing full well how upset this would make many family members.

I suppose I couldn't stop her if she chose to isolate herself more and continue to damage relationships around her. But the problem seemed to be the actions after: the guilt-ridden cries she would make to Dad so that he felt he could no longer go either, not without her. She had already been the reason in the past that he didn't speak to his siblings for years, I couldn't imagine she was really going to isolate him from the other half of his family too. She knew her mother may not have many Easters left but she still seemed willing to provide the added layer of stress to her mom of worrying her daughter wasn't at this gathering. I remember thinking *you're so upset about your daughters cutting you out that your action plan is to bail on events rather than just do what they've asked: commit to recovery?* Commit to recovery and the boundaries come down. She knows this.

Sometimes we have to cut out the people we love the most, we throw hatred and resentment their way because having them in our life, in a way that is different than we want them, is more painful than not having them at all.

She had a breathalyzer installed in her car last year, something the whole family agreed had to happen. She had developed a bad habit of driving drunk. It only takes one drive to make an unforgivable mistake. We had all agreed she was only to remove it if we felt safe without it, and only after a thorough family discussion.

But you know by now, addicts, while using, will do what serves them best. I don't think they do this in an intentional malicious manner, but rather it's simply a side effect of the sickness of addiction. She took it upon herself to get it removed. This was possible since it was implemented voluntarily (she still had shockingly not been caught in action yet). She lied about when it was taken out, because she wanted us to believe she was sober that morning, and of course if she miraculously started the car, she *must* have been sober!!!! Well, not if there was no breathalyzer.

For three days after it was taken out, she went on a bender. She drove drunk, parked where she pleased, and drank in her car. She left Dad and I and the rest of the family to go through hours on end terrified she was dead somewhere. When we found her, parked up by Shirley Macey, the soccer field, I went up to the vehicle to talk to her.

As I opened the door, the smell of alcohol almost knocked me off my feet. I asked her what she was doing. She could barely form sentences she was so intoxicated. She shoved my head out of the car, shut the door, and started to drive home. She parked sideways in the driveway, went to bed, and left again in the morning before we were awake. Again, she spent the entire day in the car, parked somewhere drinking. When Dad and I went to get groceries, we saw her car parked in the same place as the night before. When we approached, she again drove away.

I was so saddened that this was her life right now. I had to do something to try to change it.

This was when I called my friends at 911 again. As Dad and I were shopping, I was just casually on the phone with the police. They immediately agreed to go find her. My hope was a license removal, not to shame her but rather to lessen my fear that she would hit a kid by the park, or anyone really. She would put a family through agonizing pain because of her behavior, and I could not be responsible for not trying to do everything in my power to stop her from making that unforgivable mistake. I didn't want her life to include yet another pain to numb. To numb through continued drug use.

When the cops arrived, she wasn't there any longer. I hated wasting their time. But where the *fuck* did she go? I had seen her there twenty minutes prior.

That night I walked up the trail behind our house which hooks up to Soames Hill, behind the soccer field. We had a weird feeling she might be at the second entrance to the park. Sure enough, there she was. Sitting in her car, drinking, avoiding life, numbing pain. She had been there for eight hours. As I promised, I called the cops back. They were on their way, so I turned to walk home so that I wasn't there to encourage any additional anger.

Guess what? By the time they got there, she was gone.

I asked them three times to confirm the location they went to, and sure enough, it was described as exactly where I saw her. I apologized to them again, but they assured me that they were just as serious about this as I was—they have no tolerance for drinking and operating a vehicle. But I just didn't get it—I know for a fact she didn't see me. I know she didn't know I had called 911 twice that day. I know she wasn't aware they were looking for her.

Did she seriously just get spidey-senses to get out of there at that exact moment?

I remember getting flashbacks of the time in North Vancouver I tried to get her license suspended. By the time the police found her in her car, the engine was cool and the keys were not in the ignition. Despite her extreme inebriation, no consequences were implemented. No license removal. Not even a fine.

There's just something about the addict that encompasses the sneakiest behavior I've ever witnessed. I have never in my life encountered another human being that has escaped so many consequences. I have friends that have received a DUI for simply sleeping in their cars with the keys in the ignition, trying to do the right thing by choosing not to drive home after a party where there was consumption of alcohol. They seemed to get this one-off DUI for something rather innocent, yet I can't seem to get my mother caught with one when I actually try to. Amazing how that works.

She returned home late that night, never found by the cops, never caught in action. And I just went to sleep telling myself, *maybe tomorrow.*

Taking the car out was a frequent occurrence. The biggest issue was of course the intoxicated driving, but there was also the frustration of taking the shared vehicle away from the home. My dad was finally able to drive again (which I describe in the next few pages) but constantly found himself without a car. I didn't mind if she took it for a day to get stuff from Costco or have it for a couple days to visit her mother in town, as long as she was sober. What I didn't accept, however, was blindly taking it for days on end with no plan of when she was returning home, leaving dad without a reliable way to get around. I remember feeling frustrated that she just assumed this was yet another thing I would take care of... *Beth will make sure Dad is taken care of if I leave whenever I want.* Of course I will always make sure he is taken care of, but I don't like all her decisions being based on my reliability. When I discussed this with Noa, of course she challenged me by reminding me this wasn't a conscious choice. "At this point in your mother's sickness, there is zero impulse control. She isn't capable of thinking these things through, let alone thinking about who will suffer from her decisions. You feel it's a simple decision to walk into the driveway and consider who might need the vehicle if it's taken away, who you might be inconveniencing, and whether you should do it, but you are wired differently. You are a Mac and she is a PC. You are just simply wired differently right now, and you can't make sense of one another." That definitely sunk in.

Everything was everyone else's fault. It was our fault for not managing her addiction the way she wanted us to. It was our fault for talking to each other, using the family as support, because in her mind it was all supposed to be a secret... the less people that talked, the better. I guess more talking lead to uncovering more lies and more ideas for pushing her into help. No matter what the circumstance, there was always someone else to blame.

We were constantly faced with the biggest dilemma: if we forced her into treatment by kicking her out and changing the locks, we risked her self-inflicted suicide from what she would label as our neglect. If we did nothing but happily support her half-assed recovery, we watched and enabled, and she could just as easily die that way. How the hell do you choose one of those options?

I felt again like I couldn't get away from this.

I would leave the house and worry about whether dad and her were fighting while I was gone, and whether it was getting out of hand.

I would go for a run while texting my sister and aunt to try to come up with a plan for mom. I learned it's quite difficult to send readable texts while bouncing up and down, and of course the last thing I wanted to do was send them drunk-looking texts, giving them pure PTSD from mom's history of drunk messages.

I would walk into work while texting Kat about whether to give back Mom's wallet; we didn't want her buying alcohol, but we would go back to discussing our lack of power in this disease, acknowledging she could find a way to get credit cards and make her purchases again. I would have to try to forget these conversations, or at least put them aside, as I walked through the doors to work, trying my best to put a smile on my face for my patients and co-workers that day.

I would go to IGA, scanning the aisles for breadcrumbs while I was on the phone trying to answer questions from the cops about mom's history with addiction and approximate location at that time.

I would go for a walk with a friend and put the biggest smile on my face when I saw them. I would be chatty and outgoing. I would do everything I could to ensure they didn't know that before I left my front door, I was in tears trying to navigate a massive wave of grief.

I would go to Tapworks, the local bar, with a group of friends and barely be able to focus on their voices around me. I would hear them, but I wasn't listening to them. I was there in person, but not really there at all. I was just thinking of the conversation I had with my mom before I left the house:

Mom: "I'm going to die, Bethy."

Me: "That's been my fear for fifteen years."

Me: "There's options… do you want to live?"

No response, just tears down her face. And then tears down mine.

I had put a tracking device on her vehicle. I had to pay a monthly fee for this damn device just to keep tabs on her.

I always felt like things were happening, people were talking, I was moving, but all I could hear were the thoughts in my head.

Sometimes I ask myself why I'm still trying. Even though I try to cut her out, when she needs help I'm still there. I don't get why humans have such guilt-ridden hearts. I can't imagine anything worse she could do that she hasn't already done, yet I'm still somewhat in her life. I still race over to the house to delete her accidental drunken snapchat stories as I want to protect her from the embarrassment she will feel when she's sober. I still stand up for her behind her back when anyone speaks negatively about addiction or addicts. I have my own resentments and anger with her at times, but I also have an understanding of the disease state and her lack of control because of it. I have no tolerance for other people putting unspeakable labels on addicts without knowing the people or the disease in the slightest. I'm still open to that relationship being healed over time. I've lost a lot of hope that we will ever get back to where we were when I was in high school, that best-friends-with-your-mom vibe. But I'm open to the idea that it could happen. She's missing the humility part. She doesn't always apologize for her behavior (which I've concluded is likely because of her desire to avoid the entire situation due to extreme shame), and even the odd time she does, the action piece is usually missing.

That's the thing about forgiveness. We're human. We all fuck up. Hers is more from her disease state, so even more reason to be forgiving, but even if it's not, we still all fuck up. Everyone reading this has. I have. I have fucked up big time, more than once in my life. I have done things I'm not proud of. I have regret. I have unintentionally hurt the people I love.

But at the end of the day, if those people who have caused harm say sorry and put that apology into action by not doing that same mistake again, how can you not forgive them? Isn't that all we could ever want as human beings? Accountability for your wrongdoings, and never facing the reoccurrence of it happening again? If you want more than that, I'd say you've got your own healing to do.

But that was the problem with Mom: it was difficult to keep forgiving when nothing changed for prevention in the future.

I would physically leave the house, but in reality, I could not get away from this. Immediate guilt and shame for even leaving the front door. Guilt for being out having a fun night for the first time in a long time, while my dad is home dealing with my mom in an episode, and my sister is on the phone trying to calm her down. I was sitting at the dinner table at Buono, a local restaurant, with some of my best friends, checking my phone every three minutes. I was trying to listen and engage with my friends, but my mind was elsewhere. I wanted to be present, but I could not change the fact that I wasn't. I felt like I needed to leave to go home and support.

You can't always be the safety net. You can't feel like it's your job to get home in these moments. Your dad is okay. He will be okay. You can't control your mom. You need to maintain these social connections for your mental health. And you need to find a way not to feel guilty about it. Noa's voice is in my head frequently these days.

So, I'm learning to have thoughts I tell myself when I'm in these moments, reminding myself, *I am okay. Dad is okay. Kat is okay. If Mom doesn't want treatment, we cannot change that, we cannot force her to be in our lives. This is up to her, and we have no control. We just need to continue living life and letting her be the judge of the future she wants.*

Easier said than done, I'll say that much. There is a serious battle in our heads of the frustration that makes us put our hands up and say, "fuck it, do what you want" versus the guilt that makes us do anything we can to support her, which sometimes looks like forcing her into treatment.

The household dynamics were certainly not getting any easier. Some days I felt like we were maybe moving in the right direction, but without fail, my mother would fall off track and slip into a deep relapse all over again.

I was trying to spend more time out of the house because I found this really difficult to be around. I was really feeling the effects of the caregiving toll for so long, for both parents. I was starting to feel the impacts of the last few years harder than ever. There were constant reminders of Dad's deficits, some more painful than others. And there were constant unknowns with Mom's state and recovery, whether she would have a good day, or a day where she drank and told us how awful we were. I wasn't sure how many more of those I could take.

Being out of the house meant spending more time at Brydon's house, overnight. It meant going on longer walks than normal just to extend the time away from the chaos. It meant intentionally seeing my friends more often. It meant going to write or finish emails at a coffee shop with earplugs in instead of the perfectly set up office I had at home.

So, needless to say, being out of the house was a blessing in a lot of ways. But it was also a curse. Remember back when I talked about distraction feeling good but really delaying the onset of the true processing of trauma? That part is the real curse. The more time spent out of the chaos, the more time there was to process. I had no time to process in the past, not much anyways. There was always a distraction of Dad's care or Mom's relapses. It was simply moving from one chaotic event to the next. But with more time away, there came the realization of how traumatized I really was.

I continued to have random inconsolable tearful episodes at night. I would feel fine in the day, being my cheerful self at work—although I could feel I was faking it half the time—and going out with friends pretending I was totally fine. I would even feel fine heading to bed, but then the silence and stillness would give my brain the opportunity it craved to spin with my thoughts.

I would experience the flashbacks of horrible relapses, or of moments in Dad's accident that terrified me, like seeing him intubated for the first time. I would re-live the time in the ICU as if it were real life again. I would re-live searching for my mother with the fear of finding her dead. These images played in my head continuously and the only way out was to stop fighting it. I just had to let them play for those couple hours, let out all the emotion, and hopefully fall asleep. I would get up after Brydon had fallen asleep and head to the bathroom to let it all out. I would hold the hand-drying towel over my mouth and cry as hard as I could for a few minutes. I tried the best I could to make it silent. I remember standing there in nothing but my underwear, leaning over the sink, and looking at myself in the mirror; eyes puffy and bloodshot, cheeks red, my face stained with wet tears, and I just remember thinking, *fuck you look awful, how the hell can you make this stop? You need to make this stop.* I figured if I let these episodes happen enough, ideally they would get less frequent and severe, but I wasn't sure how bad it would get before I came out on the other side.

Noa continued to tell me how opportunistic the brain was, that it would hop on any time of silence to start processing the past. She encouraged me to allow myself to process more in the day, too. I needed to focus on stopping the continued search for distractions and rather let myself just sit with my own thoughts and feelings for a while.

I needed to practice this often. I was in a routine of adding more work to my schedule, signing up for courses, planning friends' birthdays, and trying to do the "Soames to Everest Challenge" in seven days. This was all a good distraction, but I knew it was just that: distraction. Noa warned me that as you let yourself feel emotion from the past, the processing starts, and it usually gets worse before it gets better. This meant that I had a lot of pain still ahead of me, but the longer I waited to start processing the past, the longer it was going to take to start healing from it.

This is PTSD. The fact that I search for distraction in a panic, the fact that I have random outbursts of severe emotion, and the fact that I have difficulty focusing on the task at hand. This is all PTSD coming to the forefront of my life.

EMOTIONAL TORTURE: PART 2

Being away from home more often also helped me gain my sense of independence again. It made me crave having my own place, but of course the market was at all-time highs and there was little chance of that happening at that time. I was hoping the times I did spend at home would be easier to manage, given that I was allowing myself that time way. Sometimes things felt a bit easier, but for the most part it was still a struggle.

I remember feeling hopeless for my mother's recovery. Our relationship felt like it was at its worst. Her continued relapses and everything that went along with them continued to break my trust and hope more and more. I was running out of patience. I was running low on empathy with her continued relapses and avoidance of additional treatment that was undeniably needed. I was sick and tired of seeing her take advantage of my dad's memory loss and try to convince him that things weren't as bad as we described from the past.

We fought frequently. Sometimes it was when she pushed my boundary; I asked her at one time, as a means for self-protection, for example, not to get involved in my personal life, but she would often push that and ask about my friends, work, or boyfriend anyways. My heart wanted to tell her every detail, to live in the past for a minute and soak it up, but I knew it would ultimately lead to more pain. I would remind her of the boundary, and she would get upset, as if it wasn't fair to have something in place to protect myself from more hurt.

Sometimes it was how she dealt with Dad; her impatience with his memory issues or her inability to teach him valuable skills. I was onto her about this a lot—*take him when you go get gas and let him use the card, take him when you go to London Drugs and let him try the self-check-out, take him to go get the mail so he can practice with someone there to remind him of how to do these daily tasks.*

Her lack of patience was a barrier to allowing her to do this. Most times, our fights were from her addict behavior that could be nothing less than using. As I've alluded to before, it wasn't the relapses that made me angry, it was everything that came along with them: lying, denial, manipulation, family tension, and hurt.

It was May 2022 when we had our most explosive life-altering fight.

I had been feeling pretty down for weeks at that point. I couldn't pinpoint why but I think it was a collection of various things. I was still living at home at age twenty-seven. I was still watching Mom more than I wanted to. I was still putting my career and personal life last. I was still taking on the responsibility of Dad and his needs; doctor appointments, grocery shopping, getting his license back, to name a few.

This last one took almost a year. First he wanted to practice in empty parking lots for a while, then we started the process of the paperwork, and then it was time for the in-person assessments at GF Strong. Dad spent months studying, both on road and reading the driving manual online. I spent hours making mock tests for him at home. I didn't want him to fail. Interestingly enough, even though Mom was sober that week, he didn't want her to take him down for his test. When it really mattered, he chose me, because he could trust me. I hadn't let him down once in the past, and he knew I would figure out any roadblock we came across on the journey to get back his license. Mom's unpredictability made it difficult to load large responsibilities onto her, so at the end of the day, these important dates were up to me to organize.

Lo and behold, he ended up passing with flying colors, and he's arguably a safer driver than most people out on the roads, considering he passed two and a half hours of cognitive testing and one and a half hours of on road testing.

Anyways, these responsibilities were rewarding but exhausting, and it was contributing to my burnout. Dad had observed my lows and asked if I was doing okay. I told him I was unhappy lately but knowing the up and down rhythm of grief, I told him I would probably move on from it soon. He had later talked to Mom, as he was genuinely worried about my sadness. Mom, unsurprisingly with her addict behaviours, had convinced him it was just a stubborn crappy attitude rather than feeling unhappy. This seemed to downplay the severity of my mental health that I was finally admitting to. This feeling of not being taken seriously on top of my previous frustrations were enough to be the last straw for me. This led to an argument between all three of us, which later exploded into altered living arrangements.

My mother had seemingly done it again. Not only did she intentionally change Dad's perspective of my emotions that day, but she continued to manipulate me throughout that entire evening. I felt so fed up with her talking negatively about me behind my back and maliciously convincing my dad of anything that painted me in a poor light, even if it meant putting down her own daughter. It wasn't so much the words she used—technically I can be a stubborn person, but in that moment it was true sadness—it was more the fact that she used me as someone to make her addiction look less bad. And it was more about using Dad's deficits as leverage to bring him

---

back to "her side." I knew it was the alcohol talking, and the alcohol acting, but I was still angry, nonetheless.

In this particular instance, she made me so angry that I was trying to get away from her in the house, calling her a bitch and giving her the finger to her face. I am not proud of these moments whatsoever. In fact, it's beyond difficult to admit I acted like this. I have never been pushed to a breaking point with someone like this in my entire life. I suppose my explosive anger was just another desperate attempt to force her into treatment. When using, addicts really do have a way of bringing out the very worst in someone.

She asked for her house key back, and that's when I really lost it. I told her if she could convince Dad to agree to that, then she could have her key. She had come storming back to me claiming Dad agreed, and when I repeated that sentence out loud back to her (because I honestly didn't believe it), her sarcastic response was, "oh great, say it louder so Dad will hear!!!"

Clearly, she hadn't had him agree at all; in fact, I later found out he was saying, "no, absolutely not, we're not doing that" when she asked him if she could take the key away from me. At that point, I just handed over the key regardless. I was so sick of the bullshit behavior. If she wanted to end like this, so be it. Here is your damn key.

Dad tried to get out of bed to stop the whole process, but I was already beyond raging to have a calm conversation about it at that point. She had him strategically come out when I was at the height of my anger, and I was giving her the finger. Of course, this made him angry. She pulled him back and said something to him, of which I could not hear, and next thing I knew he was screaming at me.

Back to the red-in-the-face screaming that he's only done when she's pushed her addict ways upon us. I was standing in the kitchen scream-crying, hand over my mouth, shaking. He was past his point of control, another brain injury deficit, and my mom just stood there watching. She "tried" to pull him away but mostly she seemed to just amuse herself with the chaos she had just created. The sickness was all too real.

I will never understand how she does that. She was able to make Dad and I fight with each other, yell at each other, and I don't think either of us ever knew why. We had such an incredible relationship, so it didn't make any sense. She seemed to thrive off this, because the anger and tension in the room was for once not directed at her. This shouldn't be done to anyone, let alone your own daughter. I kept wondering if there were underlying reasons that explained why she needed to put that tension onto me; *is this a desperate attempt at a replacement for the drug? Does she look at me and feel I can handle the heat but if it's on her, the risk is using? Does any form of someone else hurting make her feel she isn't the only one hurt?*

I was gutted, again. All I could keep thinking was how many times I had saved her life in the past, all for just continued torture. I grabbed what I could and left in a panic. I went to Brydon's. I couldn't breathe I was crying so hard. *How did she do this to me again?*

Over the next few days, we all took time to calm down. I went back to gather more things and stuff them into my car. I had no plan, but I knew I needed to get most of my belongings so that I didn't have to return there again for a while.

When I had gone over, Dad and I had a chance to talk. We spent half an hour talking things through on the deck together. He was in tears; he was upset with me leaving, he felt awful, he apologized and wanted me to come back home. I told him I couldn't live with her any longer, or she would continue to ruin relationships around her, including ours, and I desperately wanted to avoid more hurt for everyone. I tried to remind my dad of one key point: when everyone is saying the same thing about someone, it's unlikely that everyone is wrong, and that one person is right.

When he apologized, I had no choice but to forgive him. He's brain-injured now. I know in my heart that my father would never speak to me in the way he had that day. He would never have screamed in my face. But most of all, he would never have questioned our stance with Mom, or the actions we took with her. In the past, if he walked into the room with me giving her the middle finger, he probably would have fingered her too and then taken me gently under his arm to a different room to protect me. He always knew, without ever having to hear the story, that she was in the wrong when she was using. Before his accident, he knew Mom's addiction all too well, and as much as he supported her recovery the best he could, he did not have tolerance for abuse towards his kids. This change was by far the most difficult part for me.

Before his accident, he was getting burned out from her constant chaos, and he made clear that his kids came first. One time he actually threatened her to move me into an apartment so she wouldn't ever see me again. He was so protective over Kat and I through her addiction. He wouldn't allow us to go through more pain from her disease.

But now, he's forgotten a lot of this past. He's coming into this addiction with a fresh outlook. He can't believe the stories we tell him—and on top of her dishonesty, that was enough to make him utterly confused at where his stance should be with all this. He was fully supportive of every position we took with her while she was in treatment and he was still at GF Strong, but when she came home, she was able to easily convince him otherwise.

I was beyond sad that he couldn't see this in the same way he used to. I felt like I was suddenly in this tug-of-war with her, and dad was in the middle being pulled from one side to the other. I hated that I had to convince him of these horror stories. I hated that I had to make clear to him when she was lying. I hated that I felt like I was trying to pull him to *my side* when that was never a question in the past. I was coming to accept that he would just have to re-learn all this himself at his own pace. I was constantly, and painfully, reminded of his deficits during these moments.

I later found out the entire time we were conversing on the deck, my mother was texting my sister to get me out of there, that I was "barricading and manipulating him."

Manipulation hey… you're one to talk.

It was only a simple two-way conversation. At that point it really hit me that this was all very calculated. In her altered state, she had successfully created a situation in which Dad and I were fighting, and as soon as we were working through that together, she had to put a stop to it and get me out of the house again. I wondered if maybe she was hurting from how angry I had been at her, and this was her act of defense.

When I came back to the house to gather more things, the text I received from her sitting in the living room while I was in my bedroom was "you need to leave now", claiming I was only allowed back if it was pre-arranged with her. This was a family home, and under no circumstances should I have been told to leave when grabbing my belongings for all of five minutes. I felt this was a power stance; she was hurt that I had cut her out, that hurt turned into anger, and she wanted to punish me in any way she could. She intentionally texted me so that Dad wouldn't hear her tell me to leave, since she knew that wouldn't fly with him. This was what I called triangulation.

For weeks after this, there were more episodes of suspicious behavior on her part that ultimately led to more people fighting. The fighting was usually due to intentional confusion and miscommunication. The triangulation needed to stop.

Similar to any addict, she was back in isolation-mode. She had us right where she wanted us: more people fighting, more people to look bad in an effort to take the tension off of her and her addiction.

She is shameful and feels guilty that she drinks, and she drinks because she is shameful and feels guilty. This was a vicious cycle that led her into moments of being the woman we didn't recognize. She had intentions in these moments that she would never have had without the effect of drugs. It was her intention to have Dad and I fight. It was her intention to have him think we were treating her badly when we were only creating boundaries and nothing more. It was her intention for him to feel bad for her, like she's been the only one that had been wronged. It was her intention to have me out of the house, because then there was nobody really watching her; she knew she could trick Dad into thinking she wasn't drinking, or the crying was just her upset about our relationship, or the Netflix daily was just a hobby.

She knew she couldn't fool me; I knew by looking at her eyes for two seconds if she was in a relapse, I knew that the Netflix meant a deep relapse, and I knew that her crying was just the result of drinking too much. Now that I was out of the house, she could have her addict-version of her perfect, comfortable life: drink when things get hard, and force Dad to believe she's sober. Drive when she wants, without a breathalyzer keeping her in check. Tell all the lies that her addict brain forces her to, all without her daughter there to question her behavior and help her husband see the reality of the situation. She finally had him isolated and everyone else out.

My brain kept thinking *the addict, not my mom… the addict, not my mom.*

When I was able to take some space, I thought about every single family issue we've ever had—including extended family—and it seemed they could all be traced back to her. Every fight, every disagreement, every grudge, and every ended relationship. The manipulation was not a new behavior, which makes me continue to wonder when this addiction truly started. It makes me wonder with all these experiences, if her actions were simply a reflection of her suffering, her suffering before any of us even knew about her addiction.

We have no communication with my dad's uncle's family; truth be told, they aren't very nice people in general, but I did come to find out the last verbal communication included Mom. When I found out what she had said, I actually agreed with her intensions, but her sickness made her verbalize things she should have just kept to herself.

Mom's sister mentioned that mom had always been somewhat manipulative growing up. This made me continue to wonder what her mental health was like as a child and young adult.

I remember my dad telling me she got fixated on things easily, almost obsessed, but it was always with somewhat innocent things. One of his examples was a time they were on Hornby Island, and she couldn't stop collecting clams. She was so fixated on digging up every single clam on the beach she could possibly find. Even when they had enough, she couldn't stop getting more. Maybe that's not relatable but it's not entirely normal, either.

When we went to Disneyland for a family trip, my mom went on every single ride, and her favorite ones were easily the most thrilling rides. The rides I cried after due to shear panic, she would be wired after as if it jolted her body into pure joy. This seemed odd for someone who wouldn't let her kids near the edge of any mountain due to her strong fear of heights. I can't help but wonder if that adrenaline-seeking behaviour was somehow tied to addiction, a behaviour that we never thought much of given this was years before we found out about her sickness.

I also remember my mom telling me she had to take Tylenol 3's during a bout of strep throat and severe coughing when she was just a young kid. She said she could vividly remember liking the *high* from them and asking her mom for more when she no longer had a cough or sore throat. Why was this the case in a young child? I continue to believe there was something there at a young age that paved the path for addiction later in life.

My dad's siblings were well aware of being on the receiving end of her addiction. I have been told she blocked their phone calls and deleted their voicemails, all well telling my dad they were awful siblings for not ever reaching out. Again, making them look bad helped her share the burden of being "bad."

I have also been told that they tried to tell him when one of their closet family friends passed away, they each left him multiple calls and voicemails to tell him when the memorial was. She supposedly deleted them and didn't say a word to him, and when he later found out that he'd missed this memorial, he was livid. He looked horrible for not being there. And she just shrugged her shoulders as if she didn't have anything to do with it.

I didn't want to believe these stories, but the more I experienced her actions as a result of using, the more I understood they were real.

I kept wondering *why* she would do these things. What benefit was she getting? But I would remind myself that I was trying to make logic out of something illogical. This was an altered brain; a brain that had suffered abuse and trauma, a brain that didn't know how to act without drugs, a brain that sometimes made her do things we could not make sense of. A brain that was very sick.

What husband wouldn't believe his wife telling him these things? That certain people have mistreated her, or she had nothing to do with deleting messages? He believed everything because he trusted her. But as these situations became more frequent, and as we started to hear other people's versions of these stories, we did start to question the validity of hers. And it started to become very clear to me who was in the wrong.

I sat one day, with all this going through my head. I couldn't help but wonder if there were people I had to apologize to for not believing them when they had suspicions about her. I was so looped into her addiction that I too, believed every word. It was my mother, someone who should never use me, lie to me, or manipulate me. It was hard to believe that this all came back to her. But the reality was that it did.

I always had a hard time believing these things happened. She's not a bad person, but she's done bad things. *Why?* Along with my thoughts above, I would go back to believing she had a pre-existing mental health disorder that was never diagnosed or treated. I wondered if we targeted that first if she would be more successful. Maybe if there was a diagnosed mental health disorder, medication could be prescribed, targeting the root cause, and potentially leading into a life in which sobriety was possible. We never solve the problem sustainably if we don't look at the root cause, the *why* behind using.

To numb pain. To not feel. To escape. The most common answers I got from her in regard to the reason behind using. Her fear wasn't dying in this lifetime, it was living. It was living through this grueling battle every single day.

I was back to the distraction of anger versus compassion. I had never felt so angry at a human being for the way I had been treated. But I continued to remind myself that she was terribly sick. This was not my mother. This was a dark and twisted version of her, taken over by drugs and alcohol. This was the autopilot version, the version she didn't have control over. This was the version that came out of a relapse stating she has no idea why she used this time, why she did this damage, why she lied, or why she took herself away from her family again when all she wants in life is to be sober with them. The reminder of the disease state never failed to leave me feeling heartbroken for her. The immense power of the disease made her do things she hated herself for. How incredibly unfair. She used drugs to escape unbearable emotional pain that she could not sit soberly with. I would flashback to what she would tell me sober: *I just have to focus on not drinking every day. I need to wake up, tell* myself *"don't drink today"* and do everything in my power to achieve that *goal. And then I go to bed, wake up the next day, and repeat that goal to myself again. Every. Single. Day.* I couldn't imagine putting that much mental energy into not consuming alcohol from the minute you wake up to the minute you go to bed. I felt gutted for her. But the anger remained because she continued to refuse help. But again, was she too sick to make that choice? Was there help out there that fit what she needed? And was there enough help out there that was readily available? I think the anger was simply due to my own desperate desire for her recovery. I was always between these two emotions.

My lack of focus in daily life continued. I saw clients half-heartedly and barely remembered our conversation minutes after the appointment. I went to IGA without making lists (a first for me) which caused me to buy an assortment of foods that couldn't be assembled into a meal. I got caught in conversations staring into space and not hearing the person talking to me until they repeatedly said my name numerous times until I snapped out of it. I could feel myself being diverted away from my relationships and steered towards intrusive thoughts about my mom's addiction. Not only did this change my prioritization (or lack thereof) of relationships around me, but it changed how I navigated these relationships. I had no trust in people around me when they gave me no reason not to trust them, and every reason *to* trust them. I had a hard time committing to plans, with anyone. I was always looking for an escape route from every situation with someone, preparing for the possibility of needing it. I would chase boys that were "too cool" for me, I was drawn to the game of hard-to-get (remember, I am competitive and love challenges). I let myself be treated poorly by these men, without changing my level of desire for them. The attention they gave me was for my fun-side, my appearance, my body, the fact that sex would come out of it… but it was still attention. Why did I do this to myself?

Was it a lack of respect for myself? A need to feel wanted? A need to feel desired?

You know why? (Noa's voice in my head, again.) *Because you couldn't trust the one person in your life you should trust the most: your mom. And she did abandon you many, many times which makes you think you will be abandoned by others. You can't commit to plans because you've had to bail on your plans countless times to rescue her, so instead of letting your friends down last minute, you choose not to commit in the first place. You look for an escape from other relationships because you always needed to plan for a potential escape route with her relapses: an escape route for you and your family to stay safe. You let men treat you poorly because you have lowered your expectations of how others should treat you. You craved a feeling of being respected, wanted, and desired because those are things that your mom couldn't give you while using, so you found them elsewhere. There is a trickle effect here. Your actions make perfect sense based on your past, Beth.*

She could always make sense of my behaviours and always made me feel validated.

I was distracted. I was miserable. I was irritable. Things bothered me that never would have in the past. I didn't even care much for proper hydration, good food, intimacy, you name it. I wasn't myself. I was paralyzed with thoughts. This was PTSD crawling its way back into my life.

In the days and weeks that followed, I had driven around with my car full to the brim. I felt a bit embarrassed parking at the gym, IGA, or anywhere really. I was worried what people would think looking into my car, but I convinced myself they would probably just assume I was in the middle of moving, which wasn't a total lie, I just didn't have the destination yet.

I bounced around a lot. I stayed at Brydon's for a while, but I wanted him to have a break from this as well. So, I bounced from his place to one of my best friend Maddy's, to my grandma's, to my car, back to Brydon's, to Renee's mom's house (another best friend of mine). I moved around to limit the voice in my head telling me I was a burden for staying anywhere too long. I'd never felt this feeling before. I was, for lack of a better term, somewhat homeless. That being said, I will be very clear and state that I am in no way comparing myself to individuals that are completely homeless and living on the streets. I was beyond lucky to have so many incredible friends here that all made sure I knew their doors were open. And the ones that weren't local, like my friends from university, didn't let me go even two weeks without reminding me they were there to support me. They know who they are, and they are wonderful, wonderful people.

It was incredibly difficult to continue my jobs—I had four at the time— without a stable, long-term place to set up my stuff. I thought about buying, since my dad always wanted to help us with a down payment. I considered my savings with his help, and maybe my grandma's help too. I talked to a real estate agent and mortgage broker.

But when I asked my dad about the money, it seemed he was no longer on board. We texted back and forth for a while, and all of a sudden, I was hearing my mother's voice. I don't know if she was texting on his iPad, if she was just behind him telling him what to say, or if she was just simply influencing his behaviour by describing her perspective, but either way I knew in an instant this was not my dad speaking; saying things like I'm using him for money, and that I'm lying about Mom's length of addiction being fifteen years. The fifteen years was probably an understatement anyways, but the hurtful words he was using was a form of him being manipulated. I knew this wasn't my dad.

Days and weeks had gone by, and I only continued to see a more deranged version of the dad I used to know. We hadn't spoken for a month, which was longer than we had ever gone our entire lives without communication. I remember feeling beyond hurt that he hadn't reached out. I decided I would reach out on Fathers' Day. I had bought him a nice shirt and wrote him a card. I knew I would see him that Sunday. But when I finally did reach out to set a time, the response was a firm no unless my mother was also able to come. Again, I couldn't help but hear my mothers' voice in all this. These were her words, not his. It was at this moment that I realized I had fully lost my father to this addict. She seemed to control every move he made, every text he sent, and every word he said. She talked for him and texted for him, without his informed consent. Whether intentional or not, she spent every day filling his brain with dishonesty: "Beth isn't trying with me", "I'm so sad about my relationship with Beth, I would do anything to fix it", "I gave Beth twenty-five good years, but she can't seem to forgive me for two bad ones."

She hadn't tried with me, there was no humility, she hadn't apologized for anything, she wasn't sorry or she would have tried to fix it, and it had sure been a hell of a lot more than two bad years, about fifteen to be generous. And it wasn't these years that I was intentionally punishing her for, I was just realizing I needed to work through recovering from them on my own. In this altered state while using, she had successfully convinced Dad that she wasn't sick for that long, it wasn't that bad, she was there for him in the accident, and she ultimately was the victim. And with that new brain, he believed every word of it. She had him all alone in that house without me there to constantly remind him of the reality.

I felt like he was again, a domestic abuse victim. He was like a puppet, and she was in control. I felt angry but this had turned into significant concern for his wellbeing. This wasn't him; this was a carefully orchestrated version of herself, living through his body.

This was a time I was seriously concerned not only for his safety, but for her physical, emotional, and psychological health. I think my mom assumes that I care about my dad much more than I care about her. I hope she knows this is not true. I believe she would feel this way from watching the lengths I went to support his recovery, while feeling all I did for her was tell her where to go and what to do. But what she's missing here is the immense effort, time, and energy that went into her recovery as well. The energy I put into hers simply looked different. For Dad, it was teaching him human skills and being his go-to person for his rehab needs. This paid off, as he continued to get better and better. Paying off resulted in increased motivation for me to keep going. For Mom, on the other hand, it was repeatedly rescuing her and unfortunately this occurred through 911 calls, police and paramedic intervention, family intervention, anger and sometimes threats, all through acts of desperation. This never felt like it paid off, which resulted in less motivation in continuing to fight a battle I was ultimately losing. It felt like the ways I chose to show my love for her, fighting for her to stay alive, wasn't seen as love to her, it was seen as the opposite. So no, I didn't care less. I suppose this was just showing love in two different ways for which I felt were appropriate for the given situations I was in.

My text to both parents on a Tuesday night before this big blow-out:

To Dad: *Remember you can only have 1 beer, 2 at the very most as per your neurologist. I hope you have fun! Can you text me when you're home safe from the guys' get-together?*

To Mom: *I don't think that's sustainable. Can you please find another solution that's more long term and a better chance of sobriety?*

Like I said, it just looks different.

EMOTIONAL TORTURE: PART 3

I remember feeling crazy. I felt crazy that it had come to this. That I was the one there for my dad, I was the one holding his hand for three months while he was comatose. I was the one organizing his rehab. I was the one who stayed with him until he fell asleep, and who arrived at the hospital before he was awake the next morning. I was the one who took care of him after he was discharged and dedicated the next few years of my life to his recovery. All the while, she was unable to be present due to the strong hold the addiction had on her. And then all of a sudden, she was back, full speed ahead with the intention of getting him right where she wanted him: isolated, alone, and believing her re-written version of the past. I was angry, but then again, wouldn't you want to re-write some of your past if you had the chance? To delete some of your mistakes if the opportunity arose? I was angry but can understand why she attempted it. But I was still angry. And hurt. And confused. I felt crazy.

How are we here? I remember my dad always commenting on my mothers' relationship with Kat and I; how rare it was. He would always say he had never seen any other mother have this close of a connection with their daughters. From best friends to this. *How are we here?*

When you live with an addict, they can convince you the sky is purple. I know this because I've been there. I've believed things that seem reasonable while in the household, only to be shaking my head the second I'm in public again, questioning why I ever fell for that. Not only can anyone be manipulated under an addict's influence, but Dad was much more susceptible to this given his injury, and she was well aware of that.

Taking away my key was not just removing a piece of metal. This was a symbol of a potential chance at a future between my mother and me. It was a roof over my head. It was my home. She took that away from me knowing full well how hurtful that really was.

I didn't know if there was room in my heart for forgiveness this time. I had forgiven her so many times in the past, how many times was I expected to continue? At some point there needed to be a line drawn with what type of abuse I would tolerate, even if this abuse was just a result of her using, and therefore not fully intentional on her part. I didn't know how I hadn't gotten to that place of debating forgiveness yet, but it really felt like I was finally there. I know deep down I will always forgive her, but the fact I was even questioning it this time made me realize how close I was closing that door.

I knew remaining out of the house was the right thing to do, to protect my relationship with my dad, to give a chance at a future relationship with my mom if recovery was possible, and to try to start healing myself. I made sure he knew what to do in a relapse, how to get a hold of me quickly, and how to call for help to the big guns—i.e., the police, social services, and the "react case" team we had been matched with earlier. He was well set up to try this out on his own, and he knew how to get out if he so needed it. Although I was not leaving on my own terms, I was at least able to walk away with less guilt after teaching him these "outs."

It felt relieving to get so much validation from everyone around me. I did blow up in this fight we had, I lost my cool. I was pushed and pushed for years, and I finally blew. Everything I had practiced in counselling was out the window in that moment; I was texting before thinking and saying exactly what was on my mind, to both my parents.

I was angry. I was mean in my texts. I told my mother she was dead to me. I feel nauseous knowing I said that. I hate myself for saying those words in the heat of the moment that you can't take back no matter how much you didn't mean them. But this is how upset I was. Everyone around me was angry for me, in disbelief of my mother's actions. This is what addiction creates: a person so sick they are doing things they would never normally do to others, and those on the receiving end of it feeling so frustrated they say things they don't mean, that they can never take back. It always felt like a lose-lose situation.

My work was willing to give me some time off to get settled.

Patti and Mike were beyond empathetic because they had been on this exact ride in the past with my mother, and that was when they didn't see their brother for ten years. The rest of my family was very supportive too.

Noa even interrupted me while I was explaining my texts saying, "why are you justifying this to me?" I've always asked her to point out where I was wrong, but this time she really validated my experiences and didn't say I was wrong. She understood the situation and told me my messages reflected the pain I was going through with both my parents. Not that ever speaking to someone like that is acceptable, but just that it's understandable where it came from. Like I said, addicts, while using, really do have a way of bringing out the worst in someone. And this worst side of someone is really just their love for that addict, their grief of losing who they knew through the addiction, and their desperate attempts to get them back.

The following few months were mostly bad with a few highlights. One highlight was that I mustered up the courage to move out after finally finding a place to rent in Gibsons, five minutes from my parents' house. Although I was currently still at Lisa's (Renee's mom's house), it was painful to permanently move all my stuff out of my family home. I felt like I was leaving something I shouldn't. I felt like I was fleeing something that I should never flee. I felt like I was the sane person when I lived in that house to keep everyone safe and make rational decisions.

You aren't responsible here. If your mom refuses help, and your dad isn't wanting to take further action to have her removed from the house, you can't do anything here. You need to take care of yourself and get out now. – Noa's voice is back, shocker.

I knew it was the right call but for some reason it felt really shitty. I would never live too far away. I could never leave my family to deal with this alone, but living within the same walls was unsustainable.

The bad parts were just episodes of continued roller coaster events of her addiction. The sober time got shorter, and the times she was using got longer, and more severe. This time it wasn't just severe from physical violence, but from the even more gut-wrenching verbal abuse. As I mentioned previously, I believe her motive in the hurtful words were simply a desperate strategy to take the negative attention off her, but they had gotten to a point where she was saying the most hurtful and reaction-prone things she could say to someone.

It was only last week I was on my way to the house again after Dad texted me to disclose that things weren't going well. I have always told him to keep me updated, but he often doesn't reach out for help unless it's quite bad. I was at the house within a few minutes, and it didn't take long before I was calling to have the police and paramedics join us. I met them outside and made sure they all understood the situation; that she was very sick. I did this every time because I liked to prep them with her disease state to assess how they would react. If they are compassionate, they can come right in and help. If they are judgemental, I hesitate to let them inside because what we need are strict boundaries for her from those in power positions, not more people simply there to make her feel worse about herself.

"We'll give you two options, Kirsten. Option A, you go to the hospital for detox, and we can drive you there. Or option B, you can go to jail with an assault charge," Constable Best said respectfully, but sternly.

"I want to stay here," said mom.

"That wasn't option A or B," I replied.

She turned to look at me, a look that was a mix between a glare and a cry for help.

She wanted option C: the cops and paramedics leave, and she continues living like she is without any form of intervention.

The cops repeated the options several times, until she finally chose option A.

The cops assured me they would make sure she got seen by a doctor at the hospital, and that mom would not be back that night. I felt like saying *I don't think you realize how good she is at this game,* but instead I just nodded. She did go to the hospital and was seen by the ER physician. I assume at this point the police left as they figured once she was with the doctor, she was in for the night. The ER physician offered to help her detox, she refused. When she declined treatment, he had no choice but to move onto other patients that were open to his interventions. She left and came home that night.

How do we get out of this cycle?

It's Thursday. I've cancelled my clients for the day to go manage this situation at home again. Not only am I feeling resentful for no longer making money today (bye $375) but I'm feeling angry that my day has turned into a fight-or-flight sympathetic nervous system response.

When I get to the house, they're upset at each other (go figure). Mom is clearly in a relapse, acting belligerent. Instead of having the classic fight where I say she's drinking and she says she's not, and I want to bang my head against the wall, I just ask her to do a urine sample with me to prove it.

"Maybe I'm fuckin' crazy mom, but let's prove that with a clean urine sample."

"Fine okay, I'll do that." She responds weirdly confident… but she usually does this to try to convince me of her confidence before I test her. I guess she hopes I'll call it off if I believe she's serious about knowing she doesn't have alcohol in her system. Not a chance.

"Okay great. Do you have to pee?" I say.

"I'll see I'm not sure" she says.

I go to the bathroom with her and start preparing the kit. I have to watch her do it otherwise she'll come out handing me toilet bowl water with an excited face as she can hardly wait for me to see it's "negative."

I hear her starting to pee. "What are you doing?!"

"I'm peeing!"

"Well fucking stop!!! I don't have the container yet to collect it. Can you stop peeing for a minute?"

"Ahhh I can try"

Literally just close your urethra and fucking stand up.

I race to the kitchen to grab a container and run back to the bathroom. I get back and she's done peeing. Well done, mom. Hard to test the urine when we have no urine to test.

I'm annoyed. She can tell but she's drunk so she keeps me in the bathroom and transitions the conversation into a new dark twist. She tries to tell me that Dad has been hitting her. She points to a small bruise near her eye. I can feel my face getting hot. I know his morals. I know his character. I know his heart. And my first reaction is to think *I know he didn't do this.* But how can you not take a woman saying that seriously? Would Dad's brain injury force him to do something he wouldn't normally do? She pulls up a photo from her phone of a selfie with a bruise on her cheek. I tried to ask more questions. I asked if the photo was recent, she said no and that it was from months ago. Odd. I asked if it was from him punching her in the face, she replies yes. The photo looked like a thumb print at best, not from a fist. I asked why she hadn't called the police if she's being assaulted, she said she wouldn't want to do that to him. I asked why she wouldn't go to her mom's house in North Vancouver for a while to get away, she says she doesn't want to. *Why wouldn't you want to get away if you were truly in a scary situation? Most women have fear over the man not allowing them to leave. Dad would be thrilled with a break if she went to town for a few days. This isn't adding up.* I ask mom one last time if there's anything left out from her story that I needed to know, anything that would have led to that scene. She says no. So I march out to the kitchen and sit them both down. Dad denies her accusations of assault, but he does admit he gets very angry when she pushes him, and his only "physical" acts are pushing her back when she's coming at him. He says she walked in the house with a small bruise near her eye, from falling on the driveway, intoxicated. I have witnessed her falling while intoxicated and bruising her face before. He says he tried to give her ice, but she threw it down and started taking pictures of her face instead. He tells me today his trigger was when she called him weak, told him his deceased father would be disappointed in him, and filmed him to capture his reaction. This would feel shitty to hear for any man, but Dave Nanson may be the worst person to say it to. Being called weak is something no-one has ever said to him in his life (because it's the opposite of everything he is) but topping it off with bringing his dead dad into it, not to mention the fact his dad would be nothing but proud of him, was enough to push him beyond his control. He tells me he went to grab her phone and throw it off the deck (which he somehow controlled himself not to do), she tried to stop him, and he pushed her back from him, that was all.

I look to mom and say, "so the words you said to him prior to the explosion, that's the part you intentionally left out, hey."

They start bickering. It's back and forth, it's angry and conde-scending, it's not my parents. This isn't the parents I had growing up that were madly in love. *Who are these people?* I feel like I'm going to lose it.

Mom is taking hits at him: glaring, imitating, throwing out snide remarks. I'm trying to get her attention.

"Mom. Stop. Mom. Look at me. Eyes on me. Mom. Stop looking at him. Mom sit down. Mom eyes on me. Mom. Stop."

Dad starts chuckling at my attempt to control her. "Good luck" he says.

I lose it.

"OKAY FOR FUCK SAKES! Dad, go sit in that chair" as I point to chair he usually settles in.

"And mom, sit right there" as I point to the fireplace bench.

"Neither of you say a damn word to each other right now. I'm doing the talking. There are some big issues here, clearly. Dad, you know you have to walk away when she is like this. You know not to get wrapped up in it."

Dad nods. "I know."

"And Mom, you know dad has a trigger point from this injury and beyond that, he has no control. Why do you push him to that point?"

She shrugs. She's still drunk, which means none of this is getting through.

"Okay. Here's the plan. Neither of you are speaking a word more to each other tonight. Mom – go brush your teeth and go to your room. And Dad, when she is in her room with the door closed, you can go brush your teeth and go to your room. I will be back in the morning to discuss the detox plan. Bottom line: you can't live together as it's a risk for everyone's safety."

And a risk to my god damn sanity.

I help mom to bed, as she's not able to easily tuck herself in her intoxicated state. She's mad that I'm putting the covers on wrong. I just swallow my anger and try to put them on "right."

"Bethhh whY dOn't yoU just lemeee stayy at homE, I'm fiNE" she says drunkenly, with slurred words, as she waves her hand in front of her face.

Because I'd rather stick a fork in my eye than have you two live together right now.

"Because it's not safe. Goodnight."

There goes eight hours I'll never get back.

I came back the next day with reinforcements: Kat & Aunty Jacquie. It's Sunday morning, the sun is finally shining after a long winter. It's beautiful out. I want to go get a latte (decaf, of course, no more adrenaline needed here!) and go for a beach walk, but instead I'm going to my parents for another intervention. Let's see if I can have things sorted in that house before dinner tonight. Maybe I can still catch some daylight later.

Kat: "So things haven't been going that well here, hey?"

Mom: "Ummm… I mean, it's not bad."

Don't say it, don't say it, don't say it.

Me: "So you feel like your recovery is totally managed?" – I said it.

Mom: "Well, no, not totally managed."

Oh my god it's completely out of control… why the fuck are we dancing around this?

Kat: "The only way to be sober is to leave the house and either go to treatment or second stage housing."

Mom: "I don't want to leave the coast."

Kat: "Why?"

Mom: "I mean … my garden. And… honestly, I just don't want to leave."

There's a 150% chance your garden will be fine.

Aunty Jacquie: "For god sakes Kirsten. You can't keep doing this to us. We choose you over and over again, and you never choose us. You're choosing your garden and your comfort. This family is hanging on by a thread, which is centered around your addiction, and you still can't seem to accept help. Or at the very least, leave this house so that it remains safe for everyone."

Silence. Aunty Jacquie is right though… we choose mom, and she never chooses us.

Mom: "You guys just care about Dad and not me."

Don't get mad Beth, just explain it.

Me: "Choosing to spend our Sunday morning here, arguing over the best course of action for your recovery, which you refuse to take, is not something we would do unless we cared. If we didn't give a shit about you, we would say 'go for it guys, live together, sounds super safe and happy, good luck!!!' Clearly, we care, and you know that."

I should have chosen the latte and beach walk.

Aunty Jacquie: "Kirsten, our family relationships have been all about this. My relationship with your daughters isn't carefree like it should be, it's always just about our plan for you. It's full of tension. That isn't fair."

Silence. If I get mad, she'll threaten suicide. I must stay calm and make her think.

Me: "Look, you've always told me that your marriage is the most important thing to you in the world, right?"

She nods, tearful.

Me: "Okay, so I'm telling you right now the only way you can save it is by leaving this house and going to treatment. Then come back and try again. Your marriage will wait for you while you're in treatment, but it may not survive if you stay here now."

I can see Dad nodding in agreement out of the corner of my eye.

She looks like she's considering. I think my words sunk in with her.

Mom: "Yeah I'm not going to go."

For fuck sakes.

This cycle of us trying to convince her, her considering, her not agreeing to our plan, us trying again to convince her with different wording.... this cycle goes on for hours. Every. Single. Time.

After a couple hours, we agreed on a plan that she would find some options for housing. We're back a few days later as she claimed she found something suitable. She says it's a transition house on the coast. I'm suspicious, so I do my research. I find out it's a transition home for women fleeing abuse from their homes. *What the fuck is she up to now?* Back to another intervention:

Me: "There's three problems with this option. One, claiming you're fleeing abuse from your home will have the police coming to chat with Dad, giving him extreme anxiety. Two, this isn't sober living which is what we need. Three, you are taking a bed away from a woman who may really need it. Look, if you truly feel you are fleeing abuse, go there. But if you know you are manipulating the system right now, please think twice."

Mom: "Okay, I will think of something else."

Kat: "At this point, it's either choosing treatment with your family's support, or choosing to live in this house and losing your family relationships."

Silence again. I wish that was an easier and faster choice for her.

Dad tells me he's scared to call the cops on her again because he fears she will tell them he's abusing her. I remind him he has nothing to worry about if he's done nothing. He nods. This is manipulation again. He feels stuck in a position of not calling for help because of the fear of how it might be falsely spun on him.

She wants to talk two days later about another idea. She gets on a FaceTime call with me and Kat. I'm between clients and Kat is charting in her office.

Here we go again.

Mom: "So I'm thinking of doing compassionate care with my counsellor. We are going to work specifically on managing grief and loss so I can better cope with Dad at home. So, if you just give me four to six weeks without cutting me out…"

Your mom is continuing to use your dad as a reason for her relapses, but remember, her addiction started at least a decade before his accident. Your dad is not the cause. – Noa's voice again.

Noa please, I'm in an intervention.

But she's right, I can't let that side-track me.

Me: "Mom, you're not getting this. You are unstable now. You are trying to jump from this state to managing grief and loss. You can't possibly do that without the middle piece: sobriety. You need to work on that first, THEN once you have a well-equipped brain, you work on grief and loss management. You can't skip steps, or we stay in this cycle."

Kat nods.

Mom: "So it's just treatment or bust hey…"

Kat: "Everyone has to make a choice. You are making a choice not to go to treatment. We have to then make the choice to remove you from our lives temporarily. It's too painful. We are enabling this if we don't put in some boundaries."

Mom starts crying.

Me: "Mom, you get so hung up on our verbal label of relationships temporarily ending. But let's be honest, what is the relationship here anyways? You are already so removed from our lives with the time you spend using. This isn't really that different, other than the label."

Kat: "We'll talk when you hand us a ninety-day clean hair sample. That's when we will start rebuilding our relationships. Either then, or sooner if you go to treatment."

The call ends.

These interventions make me so tried. My heart breaks seeing her cry. I feel gutted. I feel guilty. I feel like a bad daughter. I feel pain. But I know that if I allow her to continue living the way she is, she won't be living for long. The tough-love approach is the only option now.

ROCK BOTTOM....?

Mom did complete the ninety-day hair sample, and it was in fact negative. She stayed sober another month on top of this, equalling a total of four months sober time. This was quite a long stretch for her.

The relapse occurred shortly after this four month stretch. I started wondering if giving her those goals, such as the goal to be back in our lives if she completed three months sobriety, was only just that: a goal for her to complete. And once it was completed, once we were back in her life, she no longer had that intense motivation to stay on track. Slowly she would start to drink, slip out of meetings, stop working the steps, and refrain from communication with her sponsor.

Her drinking and driving continued, which meant my desperate attempts at stopping this pattern also continued. She did eventually receive her first DUI in December 2023, but not without our call. She was heading to the city, sitting in the ferry lineup in Langdale, and both Kat and I knew she was drinking heavily. We once again agreed to make the difficult decision to call the police. When I called the West Vancouver Police and told them what ferry she was heading to town on, they immediately agreed to go wait on the highway for her. I felt the usual guilt in setting this up, but I could not allow her to continue risking hurting herself or someone else. I knew this had to be done.

Cheers to another Christmas calamity.

The car was impounded for thirty days, her license was suspended for ninety days, and there was a hefty fine to be paid. Of course, in making this call, I failed to recognize the consequences after which included the work to get the vehicle back sooner than the thirty days so that it wouldn't build up another fine, and so that Dad could use the car again for his errands. After many phone calls to ICBC and RoadSafetyBC, we did manage to track down the car and bring it home.

We figured this DUI and license removal may be her rock bottom, as she repeated to us many times how humiliated she felt and how motivated she was to never have this happen again. She stayed sober for a few weeks after, but by mid-January she was back into a deep relapse. We were suddenly back in the cycle of having no more than forty-eight hours without drinking, but even during this forty-eight-hour non-drinking window, the alcohol was arguably still in her system.

The dangers that came with her constant state of inebriation continued. I was leaving my apartment three to four times in a workday, between patients, to race home to settle things down. We were engaged in family group chats from morning until evening, day in and day out, about who's checking in next and what the latest updates were with her state. It was so unsustainable that it finally led us down the path of a restraining order.

For four days before going to the courthouse, we discussed our plan of an order with Mom, in the hopes she would choose to leave the house on her own terms. I remember begging her to make the choice to go to her moms in North Vancouver so that we didn't have to witness a forceful removal. She seemed reluctant to believe we were going to follow through with this plan.

I got the following Monday off work so that my dad, my aunt, and I could go up to the courthouse in Sechelt. This was all so new to me: filling out the paperwork, talking to the front desk woman behind the glass, waiting to be called in to see the judge. We waited for ninety minutes in the hallway before being called in. When we got seated, the judge directed most of the questions towards Dad, but he did allow us to intervene briefly to help provide further explanation to help Dad answer a question. I had never in my life had to speak to a judge, so I often forgot to say "Your Honor" before or after speaking. After collecting the information he required, the judge agreed to implement the order, for one year. The words are burned in my brain:

Mrs. Kirsten Nanson must remain 200 feet from Mr. David Nanson.

Mrs. Kirsten Nanson must remain 200 feet from the house on Elphinstone Avenue.

This is in effect for one year, or until Mr. & Mrs. Nanson see a judge together to abolish.

As he read out the terms, I tried very hard not to let the pool of water in my eyes overflow and turn into tears down my face.

How did we get here.

I had flashbacks of the NA family meetings we attended at Westminster house:

"Kick them out, change the locks. Make treatment the easy choice for them. Once they hit rock bottom, they may choose to get help, but they won't choose that help if they live in a comfortable environment that enables drug use," explained the mentor.

I put my hand up in the class and he nodded at me signalling I could speak. "My mom is such a high suicide risk, that kind of ultimatum seems quite risky," I said.

"If her addiction continues, it will get bad enough that you get to a place where you make these kinds of calls, knowing there's no other choice," he replied, confidently.

I let out a slight laugh. "I will never, ever kick my mom out of the house and let her live on the street, or in a shelter. I would never do that to her."

He just nodded.

And here we are. Six years after sitting in that meeting and I'm here supporting a court order to force her to leave the house. I'm doing things I never thought I would do. I'm doing things I promised myself I wouldn't.

I cannot believe this is happening.

The three of us left the courthouse with heavy hearts. Nobody wanted this. It didn't feel good or rewarding. When I arrived home to tell mom, she again didn't budge. Before I knew it, I was on the phone with the police to discuss when to come over to review the order. It was Constable Best who showed up at the house. He called me first to let me know he was there. I asked him to wait in his car until I got there, and he easily complied. I got to the house in about three minutes.

"Welcome back," I said as soon as I walked up to his car door. I felt stupid as soon as the words came out of my mouth. My tone was a mixture of sarcasm and sadness. I guess I'm still trying to cope by making light of this fucked up situation.

You could see the empathetic look on his face.

"I drive by often and think of you guys, wondering how you're doing. I remember this case pretty well, but why don't you give me a run down," he said.

We walked into the carport to get out of the rain, and I tried to give him a brief overview of the situation before he stepped foot into the house. He listened intently to every word I said. I could feel the intense compassion from his whole demeanour. Once he gathered the information he required, he stepped inside to serve her the papers. She did start arguing and asking why she had to leave. I tried very hard to calmly explain it to her in her inebriated state.

"This house is extremely unsafe right now. We are only enabling your addiction by allowing you to continue living here like this," I explain.

"Why is it me who has to go and not Dad!" she demands.

"Because Dad is sober and working on his rehabilitation every day. You are inebriated and not working on your recovery every day. If the shoes were switched, we would be forcing him to leave. It's not Mom versus Dad, it's just whatever the safest and most reasonable option is," I say.

I could see Constable Best in my peripheral vision, nodding with everything I said.

She argued for a bit longer, but both Constable Best and I repeated ourselves until she finally stopped arguing. He made clear this wasn't a choice, this was a legal document that stated she had to leave, that evening.

She cried as she trudged around the house collecting her things and stuffing them into her backpack. I could barely watch without agonizing pain.

Don't back out now. Stay strong. I know this is excruciating, it wouldn't be normal if it wasn't. You're doing the right thing. Stay strong.

"I'm trying," I whispered back to Noa's voice in my head.

I told her I could drive her to the ferry. She refused and said she would rather walk. She angrily walked past my dad on her way out the door.

"I will never forgive you for this," she said, glaring at him with tearful eyes.

Dad looked remorseful but he simply sighed and didn't say a word.

"I will also not be forgiving you for this," she said as she turned to look at me.

"I don't know if I'll be able to forgive you either," I replied. "I begged you not to let us get here. This is traumatizing. I hate this as much as you do, trust me."

It wasn't until she was standing in the carport that she realized how dark and rainy it was.

"Change your mind about that ride?" I asked.

"Fine. I'll take a ride," she muttered.

I drove her to the ferry – it was pitch black and pouring rain. As she opened the door to get out, I looked to her and said, "please work on your recovery, Mom." She sighed, got out, shut the door, and started walking towards the waiting area. I pulled out of the Langdale ferry drop-off section and started bawling. I felt sick to my stomach. I knew our offer to stay at grandmas was just to relieve our guilty hearts from having no roof over her head, but I also knew the next step if continue drinking occurred at grandmas without the choice of recovery or treatment, was a shelter. I could barely handle the idea of her living in a shelter, but I knew she had to hit rock bottom before getting help.

How did we get here.

Is this rock bottom? I wasn't sure. Her house was... her home. This was a massive loss for her. I felt like it could be rock bottom, but I was also terrified the real rock bottom was going to be a shelter or the streets, and maybe not even then.

How did we get here.

Death is a scary, scary thing. Grief feels horrible. But it was during these days and weeks that I came to realize the intensity of pain with this type of loss. This wasn't just seeing my parents die, grieving the loss of them, and remembering them for who they were. This was losing my parents even though they were both still standing right in front of me. This was grieving all the parts I had lost in both of them. This was remembering who they used to be but looking at two new versions of them; versions I didn't want to remember them by, versions I never knew them as, versions that haunt me to this day. I kept thinking to myself *death is awful, but this feels worse.* I would have chosen to lose my mom if I knew the only alternative was suffering the abuse of addiction for the rest of my life, and I would have chosen to lose my dad if the only future was one where he would be someone I didn't recognize. In saying this, I hope my mom recovers and I'm relieved I do see some familiar parts in my dad.

We continued to go through ups and downs, riding the waves of addiction. Mom spent time sober, but it was heavily outweighed by her time using and denial of the severity of the situation. I was seeing the neuro deficits emerging more strongly than ever before: when she relapsed, she used to black-out for a night but now her relapses will leave her with severe hallucinations and no memory or recollection of the past three-to-four days, and I fear this will only get longer. This concerns me for her overall well-being.

When she was sober, life felt so good. She was happy and outgoing, being her busy-bodied-self. She would have us over for dinner and be the light of the conversations again. Talking to her was such a joy. I would see things around the house that showed me she was in a good place: the garden thriving, the house clean & tidy, the laundry folded, the fridge organized, her gift bag (a bag she kept for gifts she thought of for other people) full, and of course, the licorice she would keep lined up on baking trays on top of the piano (she claimed it helped them "dry out" so they were chewier and more enjoyable). I saw the mom I remembered and love this person so much. We hadn't seen her with any substantial sober time since the court order and removal was made. I was getting further and further away from hoping I would ever see that wonderful side of her again.

I was still brainstorming solutions to keep her sober for life, but I knew in my heart there was nothing I could do anymore. There was nothing I could do that I hadn't already desperately tried.

My dad continued to have multiple medical appointments, even three plus years later there was still lots of follow up for him. Some were on the coast, but many were in the city. Some were even unnecessary, like when he wanted a re-evaluation of his shoulder, hoping for a possible answer of surgery when the orthopedic surgeon told us the year prior that surgery was out. I knew it was important to him to have this confirmed again, and it was important to me to support him, so we went through the motions of the re-assessment: family physician appointment → referral for X-ray → X-ray appointment → X-ray results → back to family doctor for referral for CT Scan → CT appointment → CT results → back to family doctor for MRI referral → MRI appointment → MRI results → back to family doctor for referral to orthopedic surgeon → see orthopedic surgeon, who then has all the results to make a decision. We continued to see Dr. Aghakhani, dad's outpatient neurologist and epileptologist, who we greatly admired for following us for so long. I took him to every single appointment, making sure we did everything we could to minimize the deficits. He was also getting some of his foundation back with this addiction; he was able to identify relapses better and create some healthy boundaries which brought him right back to his protective-father role. He remained strong in court that day, but I knew he would forever have a hard time with the tough-love approach, especially when he feared her death so often.

The worst part about these boundaries was that when mom was away, whether that be treatment or a family members' house going through detox, my dad's life got so much better. It's awful to say, and it pains me to admit, but it's true. If she's sober, his life is undeniably better with her in it. But if she's using, his life is so much worse – he's isolated, frustrated, and anxiety-driven all the time. I was like this too when I lived with her. It inevitably creates a situation in which he loses a lot of the skills he had gained, tracking backward in his own recovery. Aside from his own recovery, it disrupts his everyday life: his decisions, his plans, his emotions. He can't commit to a weekend plan away because he fears leaving her alone will result in a relapse and a future full of guilt for him. And when she is forced to leave, he is free. He puts everything I previously practiced with him into action. He rides his bike again (which still shocks me), he gets his groceries, he learns how to cook, he learns how to refill his prescriptions, he makes his own appointments, he voluntarily collaborates on work ideas with his incredibly talented colleague, Matt, and most importantly: he is connected to others. He sees family and friends often, which makes his life so much fuller. He is free. We are all free. That is the addicts' impact on the lives of those around them. This isn't my mom. This is the addict.

I was forced to remind myself every day that this wasn't the people I knew from the past. This wasn't really my mom, and this wasn't really my dad, at least not as they once were. I felt like I was a long way from acceptance, but I knew I had to start coming around to the fact that this might never change. I knew I might have to just simply remember them for who they were and try to cope with these new versions the very best I could.

I am still scared of the lows to come. I still cringe when Kat or Aunty Jacquie call me, preparing myself to hear the news of her death before I slide my thumb across the screen to answer. I still panic if I haven't heard from Dad in a few hours. I still feel a desperate need to drop by the house unannounced to get a true picture of the reality within those walls: how he's really doing, if she's illegally come home. I still tense all my muscles as I walk through the house she's in, preparing to see her in that unconscious state, my brain planning the emergency protocol I will follow if that's what I see. I even do this when I walk through a house she's not at, like the family home currently, because my brain just whispers to me *you never know.* I know things will get worse mentally before they get better, but I am prepared to go through this. I am willing to let the pain sink in knowing I will come out better on the other side.

Because I am still very much living this story, the ending is unknown. All I can do is hope the worst is behind us, accept where things are at now, and trust that the best is yet to come. I can hope my mom gets healthy, and hope there's some chance of getting back to the close relationship we had in which we were best friends. I crave that love, but until the recovery is stable, I feel I should hold boundaries to protect myself from more devastation. In addition to protecting myself, I hope these boundaries will help nudge her in the right direction of getting the help she needs, so that I can finally have that future with her I've being longing for. I still don't know if boundaries are the right call, so maybe I need something in the middle to strive for: light boundaries for self-protection but easing off to avoid throwing undeserved resentment towards her for something she can't control and to improve her quality of life by sharing some happy moments again, increasing the chance of her success. I hope she can get healthy. And as she knows, counselling is always on the table – no matter how much pain I'm in, I will never turn down an opportunity to work at this together. I believe that spending time working on our relationship is not time wasted for either of us, but I will wait for her to be ready to come into these sessions vulnerable and honest. As for my dad, I just hope he gets closer and closer to the pre-accident version of himself, because that is just simply my favorite person on earth. What's of most importance is that I need to accept that these cycles might be part of my life for years to come. But that's really all I can do, is hope. Hope and accept.

I love you, Dad. I hope you continue to recover like you are. I never want it to stop.

I love you, Mom. I miss you terribly. I hope you choose to live. I hope you choose to live before that choice is taken away from you. I am so sorry this happened to you. Although you never chose your addiction, I hope you are able to choose life. I hope you are not sick enough where that choice is gone. You can have an incredible future; it's waiting for you. Please, choose to live.

The next couple of sections are a collection of valuable lessons I've learned along the way, and my personal reflections based on where I stand today. I strongly encourage you to read them, as they are a large part of my story. I want you to know why I wrote this book, and this is something you will find out in the next section. I hope what I've written next, in addition to what you've already read, will fulfill every curiosity and expectation you had when you first picked up this book.

To every family member, friend, or acquaintance of an addict or brain injured patient, or to anyone suffering with their own mental health, I give you the utmost empathy and respect. You are doing the best you can, and that's all you can do.

MY REFLECTIONS, MY TRUTH

At the end of the day, we just don't know the kind of daily struggles someone else may be dealing with. Let's not forget that anything can spark a trigger, for anyone. And I bet you wouldn't know most of what's going on in someone else's life.

I'm trying desperately to get my old life back. I want to be the girl I used to be: vibrant, fully of energy, and always able to make someone laugh. I miss that girl. I feel bad she's been lost in a spiral of trauma. I feel frustrated that she has let these circumstances get the best of her at times. I feel guilty for not pushing her more to get back to that old self sooner. I feel like I let her down by avoiding help for so many years.

But it's never too late and I believe it starts with small changes.

I've put more focus back into my career. I have more energy working at my current interdisciplinary clinic; I am more engaged with clients that I see, whether that be related to sports, prenatal, digestion, diabetes, heart health, or general healthy eating, to name a few. I've had interest from employers for some specific gut health dietitian jobs, one being The Tummy Clinic, a virtual based start-up clinic in BC, who has asked me to be their sole dietitian. I now have an online virtual gut and IBS private practice running. In this practice, I've created an online course for those suffering with gut issues. It contains step by step modules, videos, resources, handouts, workbooks, recipes, meal plans, shopping lists, and downloadable infographics, all of which I've created from scratch. I'm looking to add additional gut and digestive health courses online, and I've already started one for bloating. I've also now started to work at Coastline Health and Performance, a clinic on the coast where I see my physiotherapist and chiropractor. This has provided me an opportunity where I can bring back my sports nutrition interest and work with some athletes again, as well as help members of my community improve their general health through nutrition. I have started working with sport teams on the coast, helping to provide young athletes with proper sport nutrition knowledge to achieve their performance goals. I am a mentor and preceptor for the UBC Dietetic and pre-Dietetic students. This has given me so much joy being able to give back as well as teach students, something I have always been extremely enthusiastic about.

I've brought my athletics back into the picture. I'm back to playing soccer, and my god it feels good to get touches on the ball again. My dad will come watch because it's a way for him to still keep the sport in his life, and because he knows every part of the way I play is a reflection of his incredible coaching many years ago. He's still talked so highly about by the soccer guys at drop-in; I always hear "Dave Nanson would have got that" if someone misses a goal. I seem to be given this automatic level of respect when people find out I'm his daughter. He is just so highly admired in this community. I'm also feeling motivated to get back into triathlons, so I've been looking online for a race in Spring of 2023 to sign up for.

I'm playing piano again. We did lessons at a young age, but I didn't have time to continue in later high school years when my sports left little room for other hobbies. Because I learned how to read notes, it's something I can pick up easily again. It's amazing how therapeutic music can be.

I got word that the TBI research paper we wrote in my internship—pre-dad's injury— is getting submitted for approval to a paper, *The Canadian Journal of Dietetic Practice and Research.* This means we may be published, which feels like an accomplishment I never thought I'd have.

I'm starting to consider reading books again. I was so used to textbooks after university that I hated the idea of reading for a while. I'd like to learn more about addiction, stress, grief, loss, trauma, and PTSD. Although I don't quite know how yet, I'm brainstorming ways to support these communities, whether it be addiction treatment centers or communities like Vancouver's downtown east side. It's not fair, our system is broken. I want to hear other peoples' stories. I want to understand this disease deeper. But most of all, I want to somehow be a part of helping them where I can. The book at the top of my list to read currently is *In the Realm of Hungry Ghosts* by Gabor Maté. I've been waiting to read it but wanted to publish this book first. He is an incredible voice in the addiction world, a true leader and advocate.

I'm in counselling on a biweekly basis trying to work through the past. I am facing the trauma head on and accepting the pain now in the hopes of creating a brighter future where I can live more in the present.

I am booking appointments for Neurofeedback and Eye Movement Desensitization and Reprocessing (EMDR) to put my best efforts forward in managing anxiety and healing from past trauma and PTSD. I never thought I'd be sitting in appointments with wires glued to my head, watching screens while the professionals observe how my brain interprets changes to light, movement, and sound. I'm proud that I'm taking the difficult steps to book these appointments.

I'm putting effort in to maintain all the important connections I have with people around me. This includes family, members of the coast community, and friends: friends from UBC, rowing, dietetics, work, soccer, and of course, the large group of friends from the coast we've had since high school that are like family to me. These are my people, I keep them close.

I am changing my perspective on my emotions. I tear up more easily now, at things I never would have in the past. Last week I watched a Tik Tok of a young woman singing, her voice was incredible. She then disclosed she had lung, liver, and spine cancer. I started crying. I don't even know her. My patient at work the other day opened up about her father and brother passing away, within the same year, months apart, and I broke down again. I feel people's pain stronger than I ever have in the past. Noa is teaching me to see this as a positive thing, not a negative "weak" thing as my genes tend to whisper to me. "This is a beautiful thing" she says. Slowly but surely, I'm starting to believe her.

I don't know that my mother will survive this addiction. I'm trying desperately not to get my hopes up in an attempt to grieve less later if the worst does happen. But I think I already know the immense grieving will be inevitable. She is a high suicide risk. Any relapse could be her last, in a good way or bad.

I don't know that my dad will ever be as he was before his accident. I grieve this every single day. But shit happens in life, freak accidents occur, phone calls arise with news that takes your breath away. And in the spirit of looking at the bright side: he's alive, he's functioning, he's constantly improving, and his humor hasn't changed one bit. For this I am grateful. He's my biggest inspiration.

At eighty-four thousand words later, you are here, and you have read my story. But I want you to understand why I wrote this book.

I didn't write this book for a pity party. In fact, that's the last thing I would ever want, and it took me a long time to decide to publish. I didn't write this book to compare traumas and complain about the severity of mine. Everyone experiences trauma, they just don't talk about it.

I didn't write this book to suggest, through their sometimes-appalling actions, that addicts are bad people. I didn't write to encourage their cycles of guilt or shame. In fact, I should acknowledge that

I don't use the term "addict" to put an unkind label on anyone, but rather to describe the version of my mother I don't recognize. I didn't write this book to cause any harm. I wrote this book to increase awareness; these good people are sick, making us perceive them as bad. Regardless of every gruesome story I told you here, and regardless of my moments of pure anger, I still stand by my words that my mom is a good person, a good person that's actions are controlled by her disease. A good person that's incredibly, incredibly sick.

I didn't write this book to expose some nasty details of my private life: my mom's sickness, or my dad's injury. I wrote this book to try to stop the stigma of addiction and mental health. Hiding the sickness and pretending everything is fine is what my family did for *years and years* for the purpose of protecting a loved ones' privacy and dignity.

But the more I thought about it, the more I realized that if I go along with that forever, not only do we avoid support, but we actually promote the stigma of addiction and mental health—that it shouldn't be talked about, that it shows some form of weakness, that you can overcome it without any assistance.

This is all wrong. And I want to change how we look at addiction and mental health. We need to talk *more,* judge *less,* understand *better,* and support *stronger.* The only way to break this stigma is to *normalize* it. These are diseases just like any other, so why can't we treat them like any other?

I wrote this book to give anyone else a feeling of ease knowing they aren't alone in whatever mental spiral they find themselves in. I wrote this book to give my main tips for overcoming trauma— I know how ugly it gets—I know how irrational anxiety can be, I know the lack of control over panic, I know how bad behavior can be influenced by pain, I know how scary it is to be on the brink of, or fully in, depression. And I want you to know, there are solutions. I want you to know there are ways to dig yourself out, and I want you to know you are valued and loved enough to fight for yourself. I want you to know you are not alone. I want you to know that I see you, and I know you can do this.

So let's talk.

This is my story.

What's yours?

MY LESSONS & ADVICE TO YOU

What do I take away from this time in my life? It's ongoing. It never stops. But I have learned a lot about myself during this ongoing process. There are many things I wish were different, that I wish hadn't happened, but there are also many things I'm thankful for.

I've learned lots going through this process. I've learned that the trauma is ongoing. I've learned that I will easily exhaust myself for the rest of my life if I don't find strategies to manage it. That I can't change the past, I just need to deal with the present and do better for the future. That I can't go back in time and prevent injuries, I just need to support where I am now. I ran for years and years before realizing I was going in circles. I've learned that I can't control everything, I can't fix everyone. I can't change some situations I find myself in, but I can adapt and accept where I am, and make goals for where I want to be.

You can find ways to cope and ways to continue moving forward. I had continually forced myself to believe that I would fix an addict, I would have a huge impact in making them see they want to recover, I would be the reason they stop. No one will fix them. Only they can fix themselves, and only when they want to. Spoiler alert, that may mean they haven't hit rock bottom yet. The game of chasing may not have been worth my mental health, but I have to forgive myself there because I really felt as though anything was worth saving my mother; screwing up my mental health was worth it if she recovered… which, is probably true, but there was and is no way to predict the recovery.

It took me *years* to come full circle on that point and accept that I have no control, I will not change her, and my constant worrying and attempts at controlling her was only really hurting me. It wasn't helping her, it wasn't helping the situation, it didn't change what she would do or say, but it absolutely made me feel burnt out like I've never felt.

With trauma, this issue isn't just simply moving on and forgetting the past. It's accepting you'll never forget what happened, knowing it will sneak up behind you in the most unexpected ways, but learning strategies to *cope* with it and live with it. That's how you take care of yourself, by learning how to cope.

So, with that being said, I have fourteen small snippets of advice, things that I have clung onto the most. I hope they can help my readers with their own traumas.

1. **Accept what you cannot change.** Accepting what you cannot change is beyond a difficult task. It takes extreme patience, understanding, and coping skills. I can't change the fact that my mom is an addict. I can't change that she comes off disinterested, annoyed, unable to focus, irritable, high, drunk, whatever it is. I can't change her behaviors, and I can't chase her for the rest of my life, only to continue to be disappointed. I can't change that my dad had a terrible accident. I can't change that I don't know exactly what happened to him. I can't change where he is at in his rehab, and I can't change his deficits. These are the things I want control over. I'm type-A so I naturally want to organize and control everything. But I can't change these events. And I can't change the past. So, my only hope is the

future. This is where I turned to counselling to be one of my saviors.

2. **Seek professional help**. For YOU. Take it from me, the girl who started long-term counselling fifteen years late because she thought she was *better* than that, she thought she was *fine* and could *walk it off*. Don't get to the point where you have resentments, like I did. It was so bad that if I saw anyone with a decently functioning family, or life in general, I would think *fuck you* in my head. Young girl having a coffee with her mom and laughing like I used to with mine? *Fuck you.* Daughter playing soccer with her dad like I used to with mine? *Fuck you.* Grandma playing with her grandkids? *Fuck you, that could have been my mom with my future kids.* Family get-togethers where everyone is happy? *Fuck you all.* Parents complaining that their kids are difficult or frustrating? *Fuck off, you have no idea how difficult it could be. I still feel having the four kids I've always wanted would be easier than managing my two parents and their conditions.* Friends going traveling without a hesitation? *Fuck, I wish I could go for a vacation guilt-free without the fear of what I was leaving behind.* Awful, I know, but I never said this was logical. In fact, I said it wasn't logical. I'm being honest. This is why I needed help. Noa reminded me that this wasn't anything to do with those people, but rather a longing for that care-free life I once had. I never want to go back to the place of resenting people for having what I once had and lost. I never want to be the person who can't be compassionate with others because I feel their problems aren't real problems. I don't want to be that person and I need to work hard at keeping my compassionate side close with me. I challenge you to be better than that. This isn't a sprint, it's a marathon. Do the

counselling. Everyone can benefit. You will need it. Start early. Start now.

3. **Write things down.** I love this one, and anyone who knows me reading this will laugh right now. I write everything down. There's like three hundred notes on my iPhone right now. For me, it works by getting it OUT of my brain and ONTO another area. I can tell myself at that point that it's THERE—in the notes—and not up HERE—in my brain—and it allows me to stop ruminating about it. This especially helps if it's on a "to do" list or a "don't worry about these things because…" list. When I'm in my logical brain, I write the reasons why it's not something to fuss about so that when I'm in my illogical/anxiety brain, I can refer to my notes and remind myself why not to worry. It really does help.

4. **Choose your battles and separate yourself from the situation as much as you can.** As for an addict, it may take you years to realize you can't change them, like it did for me, but once you do, you can remove yourself from that burden. Tell them you love them, that you will be there and drop everything in a crisis or emergency, that the door for a future relationship is open, but that you refuse to go on like this. I had to remind my mom that I love her, that I will be there in a crisis no matter what, that I'm still—somehow—open-minded for a future relationship, given a lot of effort on her end. But after fifteen years, I refuse to go on like this. I will be your daughter again, and only your daughter. I will not be your mom, your dad, your leader, your guider, your counsellor, your coach, your psychiatrist, your teacher, your social worker, your sponsor, or anything in between. *I will be your daughter.* And if it's any of those other relationships, no thank you.

Until we can be a mother-daughter duo again, we have no relationship.

It's painful to say this, I know, trust me, but you can feel good about saying it guilt-free if you are also saying you are open to a good relationship in the future. *I will be your daughter.* You want it, but you have standards now for how it looks. And that's okay. Ball is in their court, and you just have to hope they can want that good relationship enough to surrender to the power of addiction and make the right decision to get help. As for a brain injured patient, separate yourself from the burden of feeling their future is in your hands. Do what you can to support them, but don't let yourself burn out like I did. Sometimes you will lose your mind at them, and then you will feel bad. It's tricky seeing someone different in the same body. Accept them for where they are at, get help with coping strategies, and continue to be grateful they are still with you and can still improve over time. Separate yourself from the situation. Choose what is worth fighting and forget the rest.

5. **Move your body**. When we exercise, we release endorphins, those feel-good hormones, which help relieve the body of stress and pain. They actually work similarly to a class of drugs called opioids, relieving pain and producing a feeling of euphoria. Wild, hey. Move your body in a way that feels good for you, whether that's running, the gym, yoga, walking with a friend, pilates, hiking, dancing, you name it. I'm not telling you to start training for the Gran Fondo, I'm telling you to find something you love—if you enjoy it, it will be easier to keep consistent, and this is when you will see the real benefits.

6. **Fuel well to nourish your body and mind daily**. What we eat can have a huge impact on our physical and mental

wellbeing, and I'm not just saying that because I'm a dietitian. Of course, you can still have treats. In fact, I encourage you to have treats, but consider adding foods to help energize you too. I know with stress, sometimes our appetite is reduced, but not eating enough can actually impede our body's ability to recover from trauma. We need calories to replace any activity we do in the day, as well as just for the energy it takes for our hearts to beat, our lungs to breathe, our digestive system to function, our brains to think, and so on. So, if we don't add calories above what is needed to replace calories burned, not only do we impede healing, but we don't actually have enough calories to continue allowing things like our immune system to function optimally, leaving us to get sick more often and be less able to fight it off. Give yourself the nutrients you need to heal.

7. **Make time for meditation**. I used to think meditation was really weird; like, you really expect me to sit with my legs crossed and hands out, listening to someone tell me how to breathe? I know how to breathe? I *thought* it was weird until I actually gave it a shot. A wee bit frustrating at first, but wow does it ever work. Focusing on one thing, and one thing only—like your breath—allows you to forget about everything else, even just for that short period of time. I realized my body would relax in places I didn't even think were tense – my jaw, my shoulders, my butt??? It's only when you're reminded to relax every muscle in your body that you realize how many muscles are tense. And although I can barely keep focus for the short ten minutes, I know it will get better over time. Give it a try, I dare you.

8. **Explore vulnerability.** It's uncomfortable, but sometimes we have to get comfortable being uncomfortable. That's

where growth happens. Vulnerability is our most accurate measurement of courage, as Brené Brown says [3]. Talk about your story, share your feelings with others, admit when you're wrong, surrender to relationships that no longer benefit you, be open to change. It's amazing how much connection we can get from opening our hearts and our minds.

9. **Continue living your life**. Sounds annoying and cliché, I know, but otherwise you will be sucked into this world of spiraling negativity. Go to your workout class, go for a walk, don't bail on your social events, keep your good friends around, make food you want to eat, go for that massage, get yourself a fucking cookie. Just do what you need to do to continue living with this chaos in the background. Keep it on the backburner and keep yourself right on that front element. If you've dealt with an addict, or a brain injured patient, I know for a fact you've put yourself and your own needs last over and over and over again. Not anymore. You can't take care of anyone if you don't take care of yourself. You're in the spotlight now, give yourself a good show.

Noa told me again and again how I always sounded like a mother: *You talk like a parent talks; you are revolving your day or week around making sure they are taken care of first, you sound like a burnt-out single mom.* I finally understood that if I don't deal with my trauma, talk to professionals, address underlying anxiety and depression that was a result of addiction, grief, and loss, then I ultimately continued to let it control my actions and behaviors. It's not about running away from these emotions; it's about facing them head on and dealing with them. This doesn't make them go away, but it allows you to cope with them when they arise.

10. **Advocate for change.** Use your voice, stand up for what's right, write letters, send emails—whatever it takes to change our system. Both my parents taught Kat and I to stand up for ourselves from a young age. We were taught how to manage adversity and come out stronger. They taught us not to give up, but more importantly, how to do a job well. I remember Dad always saying, "don't do the job half-assed" with anything we would do, even if it was just sweeping the driveway. This really stuck with me. I know there are so many others that feel at a loss that mental health isn't taken as seriously as it should be in our current system. We need to push for more treatment options for addicts. We need to decriminalize drugs, regulate them in a safe supply to prevent more deaths. We need to normalize needing help for mental health. The more people that speak up, the closer we get to change. Don't be shy.

11. **Forgive yourself for past wrongdoings.** I'll say it now and I'll say it one hundred more times: sometimes good people can do bad things, and still be good people. The key is that you are accountable for your actions—whether to yourself silently or others out loud—learn from your mistakes and strive to not make the same ones again. I will admit I've done things I'm not proud of, and I know every one of you has as well. But I have made an effort to understand why I did those things and have made changes in my life to ensure I don't do them again. It's interesting learning about why we perform certain actions. I've learned that it's almost always a result of pain, grief, or loss. Pain can push us to do things we wouldn't normally do, to make us unrecognizable to ourselves, to live through consequences and cope with regret. But let's remember regret means you have a

heart—you know you did something wrong, that's the difference between someone who has no regret and someone who has regret. The one who doesn't have regret probably isn't a great human and will continue to do harm. The one who has regret is a good person who will learn from their mistakes and no longer cause harm. An apology can go a long way, especially if the party hearing it has compassion and understanding for mental health faults. Forgiveness usually doesn't come in isolation; we have to accept that anger usually tags along with it. This is why forgiveness is difficult, but also why it makes you stronger. So, for me, for you, please: forgive others, and forgive yourself.

- I have to forgive myself for not believing anxiety was a real condition, and for judging those who said they were sufferers before I understood the condition's power.
- I have to forgive myself for ending relationships or friendships in the heat of my mother's addiction when my brain told me I had no capacity for those things at that time. I felt I was dragging people along this ride with me, which wasn't fair to them.
- I have to forgive myself for putting my needs to the side over and over and over again.
- I have to forgive myself for dropping an online business course that cost six thousand dollars, that I ended up not being able to manage with life at home. It takes a lot for me to quit something… A LOT. And I hate that I wasn't able to continue this course; it eats away at me, but I guess Noa would be proud of me for listening to that tolerance level that was being abused.
- I have to forgive myself for getting physical to get Mom to treatment: pulling her out of the house, putting her in the

car… I need to understand I did it for the right reasons, but it's hard to accept this.

- I have to forgive myself for adding her to the "do not allow in" list at the VGH ICU. I feel guilty but I know it was the right thing to do at the time. I couldn't allow her in under the influence; I knew that one accidental pull on one of Dad's tubes could impact his chances of survival and I just couldn't take that risk. I knew it was better for her recovery to be in treatment, as seeing Dad in that acute state was causing her to spiral more. I felt sick that I needed to protect my dad from his own wife, but this was the reality at the time.

- I have to forgive myself for kicking her out of grandma's house when things were bad. She couldn't live there with her behaviour and I knew it would break grandma to ask her herself. I thought it would be easier but seeing her pack and walk up the driveway with her backpack was traumatizing. I didn't know if that would be the last time I saw her.

- I have to forgive myself for acting outside the law, being part of a situation in which tests were falsified.

- I have to forgive myself for helping Dad change his power of attorney from Mom to me. This felt sickening, but her mental state had no control, and she was draining the accounts. My dad needed the assurance he would have finances for a future. Another thing I had to do to protect him, to protect us, but it pained me.

- I have to forgive myself for the countless times we tried to get Mom certified, with the end result being a warrant from a judge to get her taken out of the house in handcuffs and taken to the psych unit. I knew it had to happen, and

I knew it saved her life that week. But I hate that my sister and I had to be part of forcing it.

- I have to forgive myself for not being better at walking away before I said something I didn't mean. Always, always walk away. Don't text or email back right away. Think, process, take time. I guarantee you will avoid much conflict going down this path, and I know this from years of NOT doing it.

- I have to forgive myself for cutting off communication with my own mother at times, in a desperate attempt to lessen the amount of cortisol in my blood.

- I have to forgive myself for wondering if life would just be easier without her. I have felt sick for my brain even sitting in those thoughts. I've grieved her death so many times I've lost count. At least since I was fifteen years old. I guess I accepted it a long time ago, because I lost her a long time ago. It's been exhausting so I understand why I thought that, but I have a hard time forgiving myself for wondering it.

- I have to forgive myself for seeing my career take a hit due to life chaos. I love my outpatient clinic dietitian job, I love the team, I love the other dietitians, and everything about it. But I was getting so burnt out that I found myself distracted constantly.

- I have to forgive myself for letting trauma get the best of me, and for becoming someone I didn't recognize at times.

12. **Don't fear believing in a power greater than yourself.** I didn't grow up in a religious family. I never went to church or learned how to pray. I think I always knew some people believed in God, and others didn't. I just didn't have time to really think about whether I did or not. I feel I sort of sit in the middle, I wouldn't say I necessarily believe in God,

but I believe in something greater than ourselves. Maybe that is God, or maybe it's some other form of higher power. But there's been moments of questioning what's up there, moments when a "higher power" seemed evident:

- when I knew something bad was coming two days before Dad's accident. It was my birthday and I remember hating it… something wasn't right. I couldn't pinpoint it whatsoever, but I remember feeling very nervous that something bad was on its way. My gut never lies, or maybe it was a higher power warning me.

- when dad stopped seizing after Kat and I begged him for one last chance and I went to church to pray for him.

- when dad brought his arm up to my shoulder on grad day when I told him I missed him. He was unable to move his limbs or eyes that same morning.

- mom somehow surviving the abuse to her body and brain for all these years, getting chance after chance with her at a future. How she has lived through this addiction for all these years is beyond me. So far beyond me. I'm grateful she's alive, but I'm also confused as hell. It's like she has dodged every possible bullet sent her way. The number of times she had close calls where I thought *this is it* are overwhelming, too many to count. And I've always wondered if someone is watching over her, saving her life just as much as we are with every relapse. Her longevity makes no physiological sense.

I think some people are raised to believe in God, so they simply just don't know any different. But I think for others who found it themselves, I think they had a reason to find it. When you experience trauma, you are desperate for something to believe in, to come to in times of pain, to help you forgive others easier, and to protect you and your loved ones.

Maybe I'm spiritual, maybe that's the best way to put it. I don't know what I believe in, I don't pray daily and have routines, but I do believe there is something up there having influence over our daily experiences. Let's leave it at that.

13. **Hold gratitude for the things you do have; they could be gone tomorrow.** This one sounds like another cliché, but I think we've all experienced the speed at which your life can change these past few years. For my dad, it was one phone call. One phone call that I will never forget, that changed my life forever. Most accidents are like this—a car crash, ski incident, overdose, stroke, heart attack, you name it. In a matter of seconds, your life can change forever. And there's no going back.

It's difficult to live each day being grateful, to remind yourself that it could not only be your last, but your loved one's as well. It's especially difficult when you have unresolved resentments. The state of the earth makes it no easier—fires, floods, earthquakes, tornados. Climate change might get us first if we're not careful. There's a lot to be upset over, but in the big picture, is it worth it? I have a hard time with this one. Being grateful when there's so much to be angry at. But there's a lot to be grateful for, you just have to look closer. The reminder of knowing anything could happen at any time does help. Knowing I could lose my mom tomorrow gives me more motivation to be nicer, more empathetic to her, and more forgiving for the past.

14. **Create space for empathy.** I never used to carry a lot of empathy, but these events have changed my perspective. It was very easy for me to judge someone as a person from the actions and behaviors they displayed. A classic example would be someone not holding the door open for you when you KNOW they know you were right behind them.

I would take this action and silently label them as *rude, selfish, unaware, naive, entitled...* you name it. I then had the unfortunate opportunity to be on the other side of this. I was the one who wasn't thinking about holding the door for the human behind me. But this wasn't because I didn't care, or because I am rude, selfish, unaware, naive, or entitled. It was because I was too distracted with the thoughts of whether my mother would be alive when I returned home, or if my dad had come out of the coma yet. Proof that good people can do bad things; I believe I'm a good person, but I have still done bad things, and I would hate if others had inappropriately labelled me as something I am not, because of my actions, as this was a presentation of my mental state more than my character. As Edith Eger says, "It's not my identity, it's what was done to me" [4]. So now every time someone does something odd, instead of thinking *what an asshole*, I think *I wonder what's going on in their life. I wonder what kind of trauma they are experiencing to not have the capacity to do this kind gesture.* Creating this space to have empathy for someone else not only reduces the negative interactions they experience in the day, but also allows you to change your emotion from anger to curiosity and empathy. This keeps you calm and content; win-win. It builds connection with others and ourselves. And yes, some people are just assholes without an excuse. But why not give them the benefit of the doubt here? The power of pain is enormous and the resulting impact on behavior is even bigger. I challenge you to consider this the next time someone is miserable, angry, short with you, rude, selfish, unaware, naive, or entitled. These actions and behaviors may be real health conditions, not character flaws.

ACKNOWLEDGMENTS

To my dad - for your strength, courage, honesty, and fierce loyalty. For your humor that never fails to make me laugh until my stomach hurts. For teaching me how to stand up for myself and passing down your admirable qualities. Being your daughter is an honor and a privilege. You continue to be the benchmark comparison for any man that walks into my life, and that is an exceptionally high bar to meet.

To my mom – for your determination, grit, and unfathomably resilient genetics. For your strength in continuing to fight an incredibly difficult battle. Your perseverance is inspiring. For giving me the opportunity to experience you as a best friend. For making me the strongest version of myself that I will ever know. For raising me to be the person I am today. Thank you for your undeniable bravery in supporting me to share this story.

To Kat – for your patience, empathy and understanding. For your ability to manage every situation calmly, and for pushing my stubborn ass to do the same. For training me to pause before responding to texts that fire me up, giving it at least a few hours has definitely benefited the person on the receiving end. For being someone I am still constantly trying to resemble more of. Thank you for sticking this out with me, through the best and worst of times.

To my extended family: aunts, uncles, cousins, grandparents – for your continued support in this crazy world we are navigating. You all have a very special place in my heart.

To my Friends – for allowing me space to yell, cry or utilize dark humor as a coping mechanism, without a trace of judgment. For your exceptionally high tolerance in keeping me around despite the drama I've brought to the table. For your courage in always having my back, no matter what. For making me food when you knew I couldn't feed myself. For taking care of me when you knew I couldn't take care of myself. You know who you are, and your support has never once gone unnoticed.

To the Sunshine Coast Community – for your ability to beautifully come together in a crisis. Your devotion to each other is incredible. You've helped create an environment in which I actually enjoy doing errands, because I get to see all the familiar faces that always put the biggest smile on my face. I am constantly grateful for this entire community.

To my counsellor, Noa Rabin – thank you for giving me the brutal honesty I ask for, for letting me snack during sessions, and for giving me countless strategies to manage grief, loss, and PTSD. I am drawn to your perfect blend of challenging me to alter my perspective while still validating every single one of my experiences. Coming from someone who previously hated the idea of counselling, I can confirm you have helped make this one of the best decisions of my life. And for that, you should be incredibly proud.

To the staff at Westminster House Society – thank you for the work that you do every day in guiding addicts down the path to recovery. Although there were times she probably hoped you would, thank you for never shutting your doors on my mother. Thank you for always challenging her to dig deeper. Thank you for repeatedly reminding her this disease isn't her fault and for providing her with the skills and tools to overcome the past, and remain on a good path for the future.

To Dhruv – for your amazing photography skills. You had a vision no one else had and I would never have been able to get this front cover photo without you.

To the large handful of individuals who offered to read my pre-published draft – I never thought I would get this much interest. I was lucky to have three individuals read this draft and provide feedback. A special shoutout to Erin: your whole-hearted, thoughtful, and insightful comments were invaluable.

To the FriesenPress Team – although the sheer volume of red marks all over my manuscript made me want to throw out my computer and quit, it challenged me to continue working away at making this book turn into exactly what I hoped for. Thank you for the editing, design work & overall support that helped bring my story to life!

REFERENCES

[1] Sunnybrook Trauma, Emergency & Critical Care, *Ranchos Los Amigos Levels of Cognitive Functioning Scale, A Guide for Family and Friends*. Sourced from: https://sunnybrook.ca/uploads/1/programs/trauma-emergency-care/rancho-los-amigos-scale-of-cognitive-recovery-acc.pdf

[2] The Decriminalization of Illegal Substances in Canada, *A Position Statement of the Canadian Psychological Association (CPA)*. 2023. Sourced from: https://cpa.ca/docs/File/Position/Decriminalization%20Position%20Paper%20EN%202023-Final.pdf

[3] Brené Brown Podcast, Ted Talk: *Listening to Shame*. 2019.

[4] Brené Browns' "Unlocking Us" Podcast with guest Edith Eger: *Recognizing the Choices and Gifts in Our Lives*. 2021.

ABOUT THE AUTHOR

Beth was born and raised on the Sunshine Coast in British Columbia, Canada. She spent her childhood in Gibsons and then jumped between Gibsons and Vancouver while completing her post-secondary education at the University of British Columbia. She admits she has never written a book before, but felt this story was too important not to share. She feels passionate not only about revealing the true sickness of addiction and mental health, but in being a support to others enduring their own traumas. She has a good understanding of emotions such as heartbreak, grief, and loss, and doesn't want anyone to feel alone in whatever mental spiral they find themselves in. She hopes this book can be a tool for awareness, understanding, and a sense of coming together in support for those who need it. Beth is now back living on the Sunshine Coast after several years in Vancouver. She is a successful dietitian, working out of three interdisciplinary clinics as well as running her own private practice. She is currently working to co-publish a paper on Traumatic Brain Injuries. And after years of therapy, she is learning to re-balance the things in her life that bring her joy: family, friends, relationships, career, athletics, and adventure.

Printed in Canada